ASSANGE IN SWEDEN: THE POLICE INVESTIGATION

ASSANGE IN SWEDEN: THE POLICE INVESTIGATION

Authored by Radsoft and Rixstep
Edited by Bridget Hunter

CONTENTS

Preface: Twelve Hours That Shook the World   vii

Introduction: August Heat   1

Translator's Note   7

Chapter 1: The Interrogation of Sofia Wilén   13

Chapter 2: The Interrogation of Anna Ardin   29

Chapter 3: The Interrogation of Julian Assange   37

Chapter 4: The Interrogation of Petra Ornstein   57

Chapter 5: The Interrogation of Hanna Rosquist   65

Chapter 6: The Interrogation of Kajsa Borgnäs   71

Chapter 7: The Interrogation of Katarina Svensson   77

Chapter 8: The Interrogation of Johannes Wahlström   83

Chapter 9: The Interrogation of Donald Boström   123

Chapter 10: The Interrogation of Joakim Wilén   161

Chapter 11: The Interrogation of Seth Benson   167

Chapter 12: The Interrogation of Marie Thorn   173

Chapter 13: The Lab Results   181

Chapter 14: After the Interrogations   189

Postscript: Klara Kops   193

PREFACE:
TWELVE HOURS THAT SHOOK THE WORLD

WikiLeaks founder Julian Assange entered Sweden for the third time in 2010 on Wednesday 11 August. He was to give a talk for the 'Brotherhood Movement'[1] of Sweden's Social Democratic party, but he had other things in mind as well.

The Afghan War Diaries[2] had just been released, the FBI now knew about Bradley Manning,[3] and the FBI and the UK police were at the Welsh home of Manning's mother.[4]

Assange felt the heat and thought it safest to leave the UK for a while.

Julian also wanted to get publishing rights in Sweden,[5] a country known for its extreme protection of journalistic sources. Publishing rights are only available to Swedish citizens and permanent residents, so Julian planned to apply for residence as well.

Anna Ardin, secretary of the Brotherhood Movement back then, organised Julian's visit.[6] The original plan had been to put Julian up in a hotel, but hotels are notoriously expensive in Sweden, and she and her people heard Julian preferred 'incognito' living anyway; as she was scheduled to be out of town for the week of his arrival, she suggested he use her flat instead.[7]

Anna then turned over arrangements to freelance reporter and photographer Donald Boström.[8] She was supposed to return on the morning of 14 August, in time for Julian's talk.[9] Sweden's Pirate Party[10] was to arrange for Julian's accommodations starting on that same day.

But Anna returned home a day too early—Friday 13 August.[11]

Friday 13 August

Anna confronted a surprised Julian working in her flat and suggested she and he go out for dinner to discuss the delicate situation. They returned to the flat after dinner, having agreed that Julian should stay on in the flat, now together with her.[12] They had sex later that

night.[13]
Saturday 14 August

Meanwhile, Sofia Wilén, a girl previously unknown in those circles, had contacted the Brotherhood when she learned Julian would be in town, and asked for a seat for his talk.[14] She brought along her camera and wore a shocking pink cashmere jumper[15] on Saturday 14 August.

That day, Julian's talk lasted only half an hour. Julian, Anna, the Brotherhood Movement's Chairman Peter Weiderud, Swedish journalist Donald Boström, and Swedish journalist Johannes Wahlström decided to get lunch in the area afterwards. Surprisingly, Peter Weiderud also invited along Sofia Wilén to the lunch, an action that startled and worried the two Swedish journalists Boström and Wahlström.[16]

Peter Weiderud and Johannes Wahlström, during the lunch, came up with the idea of holding a traditional Swedish crayfish party (Swedish: *kräftskiva*) for Julian.[17] The party would be held in the courtyard back of Anna's flat that same evening.

Anna got to work on her mobile phone immediately, contacting people, inviting them, and telling them what they needed to bring along.[18] Peter wouldn't attend, and Sofia wouldn't be invited, but the others would all be there.

Sofia, Johannes, and Julian wandered off together after the lunch to the Haymarket Square,[19] not sure what they were going to do for the afternoon. Johannes mentioned that his parents were moving, and suggested Julian could tag along and help with moving furniture. But Sofia, who was at that time employed by a museum in the area, tugged at him as well and suggested he accompany her to her museum to watch a movie. Julian opted for the movie.[20]

The guests at the crayfish party that evening included Kajsa Borgnäs, a colleague of Anna's and also a member of the Social Democrats; Rick Falkvinge[21] and Anna Troberg[22] of the Pirate Party, who'd been planning to provide further accommodations for Julian starting that very day;[23] and the two journalists Donald Boström and Johannes Wahlström. Although Sofia was not at the party, Julian talked with her by phone later that evening.[24]

The party went on until about 03:00 in the morning.[25] Rick Falkvinge and Anna Troberg discussed Julian's accommodations with Anna, who told them that Julian was just fine where he was and would continue living with her. Johannes stayed on after the other guests had left at 03:00, helping to clean up, and he too suggested alternate accommodations for Julian, as Anna's flat was tiny in the extreme - only about 25 square metres with only a narrow bed and a minimal sofa.[26] Anna told Johannes that she would keep Julian in her flat.[27]

Some strange things happened at the crayfish party, all revealed in the testimony you're about to read. You'll read the jokes told by Anna about her relationship with Julian,[28] and how Anna offered Julian to her friend Kajsa for the night.[29]

All this after a supposed incident during which, Anna Ardin would later claim, she had been the victim of a sexual assault.

Sunday 15 August

Julian and Anna met Rick Falkvinge and Anna Troberg the following day at the Glenfiddich Warehouse pub to sign the agreement whereby the Pirate Party would share hosting for WikiLeaks on their servers. Anna Ardin came in the official capacity of WikiLeaks press contact. Also present was Pirate Party network admin Richie Olsson, who took photographs of the occasion.

Monday 16 August

Johannes Wahlström received an SMS message from Anna Ardin in which she complained about Julian's hygiene and mentioned that she washed his clothes. Johannes asks later that day if Anna is still willing to have Julian live at her flat, and she says that is it ok.[30]

In the meantime, Sofia Wilén reached Julian by telephone on Monday 16 August. Julian was on his way to a meeting with Johannes Wahlström and others in Stockholm. Sofia lived in Enköping, which was quite a bit outside the city and a long commute; so she decided to wait in Stockholm until Julian was able to meet her. She then took him home to her flat for the night.[31]

Tuesday 17 August

In the morning, Julian returned to Stockholm, and stayed at Anna's flat until Friday 20 August.[32] Johannes again checked with Anna to make sure she was still willing to have Julian live at her flat, and she again confirmed that it was ok.[33]

Wednesday 18 August—Friday 20 August

Julian continued to stay at Anna Ardin's flat, but after Wednesday Anna decided that she did not want Julian staying with her any longer.[34] At some point during the next few days, Sofia got in contact with Anna.

Julian moved out on Friday 20 August. That same day, Anna and Sofia went to the police station.

Anna now claimed that Julian had molested her on Friday 13 August, the night before the seemingly jovial crayfish party, by intentionally ripping the condom they were using. She was to tell the police she mostly likely had this used condom lying around somewhere in her flat, but had not checked to see if it was really broken.[35]

Sofia was to claim that, although Julian had used condoms during multiple sessions of intercourse with her earlier that night and the next morning, he had attempted to penetrate her one last time without a condom. She said she'd been dozing off to sleep, felt what he was doing, asked him coyly what he was 'wearing', whereupon he replied coyly 'I'm wearing you', whereupon she told him he'd better not have STDs, whereupon he told her 'of course not', whereupon they had intercourse again.[36]

Now the Swedish authorities seem to be claiming that those few seconds of partial penetration before giving her approval were in effect rape.

Anna and Sofia met Anna's friend Criminal Inspector Irmeli Krans at the police station, where the inspector took down Sofia's testimony.

In the meantime, Prosecutor-on-duty Maria Häljebo Kjellstrand had received word of what was going on before Sofia's testimony had begun, and immediately issued an arrest warrant for Julian Assange. The police were sent out to find Julian in Stockholm and arrest him.

Inspector Krans and Sofia were interrupted during the interrogation with news of the prosecutor's decision to issue an arrest warrant for Julian. Inspector Krans wrote in her notes that Sofia became distressed at this point, making it impossible for Inspector Krans to complete the interrogation, read back her notes to Sofia, or get Sofia's formal signed approval.

News of the arrest warrant reached freelance photographer Stefan Söderström at 19:52 that evening. Stefan was attending the prime minister's annual crayfish party at his summer residence in Harpsund outside Stockholm, along with *Expressen*[37] reporter Niklas Svensson. Stefan was asked to get back to town at once as Julian's arrest might be imminent, and *Expressen* wanted a photograph of the event. Niklas raced back to *Expressen*'s offices in the Marieberg area of the city to 'assist' reporter Diamant Salihu, who'd already begun working on the story. Diamant had already contacted Prosecutor-on-duty Kjellstrand to get corroboration - and unbelievably enough, the prosecutor had given it. This of course makes no sense at all, as the idea with the arrest was to detain Julian before he left the country, before he knew he was under arrest. And what *Expressen* would do was very much against Swedish journalistic guidelines: you never publish anyone's name in such a situation.

Saturday 21 August

The *Expressen* story hit the web at 05:00 Saturday morning 21 August. Despite the warrant, Julian had not yet been arrested; and at 16:48, the new prosecutor, Chief Prosecutor Eva Finné, rescinded the warrant, having reviewed Sofia's testimony and concluding that no crime had been committed.

From being publically accused of rape at 05:00 to being cleared of that same charge at 16:48—twelve minutes short of twelve hours. Twelve hours that shook the world.

But as everyone now knows, the case was reopened. And then the fun really began.

---

[1] Swedish: *Broderskapsrörelsen*; a common name for the Swedish Association of Christian Social Democrats (*Sveriges kristna socialdemokraters förbund*). An obscure Christian movement within the Social Democratic party which nevertheless can count many powerful Swedish politicians as members. The Swedish journalist and politician Peter Weiderud is the titular head of the Brotherhood, and former Swedish Minister for Justice Thomas Bodström is also a member.

[2] An archive of over 75,000 secret United States military reports on the war in Afghanistan from 2004 to 2010, published by WikiLeaks on 25 July 2010; see http://wikileaks.org/afg/.

[3] Bradley Manning is a United States Army soldier arrested in May 2010 and subsequently charged with having transmitted classified material about the war in Afghanistan to WikiLeaks.

[4] Bradley Manning's mother was originally Welsh; although Bradley was born in the United States, after his parents were divorced, his mother moved back to Wales in 2010.

[5] See Chapter 9: 'The Interrogation of Donald Boström'.

[6] See Chapter 2: 'The Interrogation of Anna Ardin'; Chapter 3: 'The Interrogation of Julian Assange'; Chapter 8: 'The Interrogation of Johannes Wahlström'.

[7] See Chapter 9: 'The Interrogation of Donald Boström'.

[8] Ibid.

[9] See Chapter 2: 'The Interrogation of Anna Ardin'; Chapter 9: 'The Interrogation of Donald Boström'.

[10] Swedish: *Piratpartiet*; a Swedish political party established in 2006, focused on reforming patent and copyright law as well as with strengthening the privacy rights of individuals and increasing the transparency of government..

[11] See Chapter 2: 'The Interrogation of Anna Ardin'; Chapter 8:' The Interrogation of Johannes Wahlström'; See Chapter 9: 'The Interrogation of Donald Boström'.

[12] See Chapter 2: 'The Interrogation of Anna Ardin'

[13] See Chapter 2: 'The Interrogation of Anna Ardin'; Chapter 3: 'The Interrogation of Julian Assange'.

[14] See Chapter 1: 'The Interrogation of Sofia Wilén'.
[15] See Chapter 1: 'The Interrogation of Sofia Wilén; Chapter 8: 'The Interrogation of Johannes Wahlström'.
[16] See Chapter 8: 'The Interrogation of Johannes Wahlström'; Chapter 9: 'The Interrogation of Donald Boström'.
[17] Ibid.
[18] See Chapter 9: 'The Interrogation of Donald Boström'.
[19] Swedish *Hötorget*; a city square in downtown Stockholm with outdoor markets.
[20] See Chapter 1: 'The Interrogation of Sofia Wilén'; Chapter 8: 'The Interrogation of Johannes Wahlström'.
[21] Swedish IT entrepreneur, founder of the Pirate Party, and party leader at the time of the crayfish party.
[22] Deputy party leader of the Pirate Party at the time of the crayfish party, becoming party leader on 1 January 2011 after Falkvinge resigned.
[23] See Chapter 9: 'The Interrogation of Donald Boström'.
[24] See Chapter 1: 'The Interrogation of Sofia Wilén'.
[25] See Chapter 8: 'The Interrogation of Johannes Wahlström'.
[26] Ibid.
[27] See Chapter 8: 'The Interrogation of Johannes Wahlström'; Chapter 9: 'The Interrogation of Donald Boström'.
[28] See Chapter 9: 'The Interrogation of Donald Boström'.
[29] See Chapter 6: 'The Interrogation of Kajsa Borgnäs'.
[30] See Chapter 8: 'The Interrogation of Johannes Wahlström'.
[31] See Chapter 1: 'The Interrogation of Sofia Wilén'.
[32] See Chapter 2: 'The Interrogation of Anna Ardin'.
[33] See Chapter 8: 'The Interrogation of Johannes Wahlström'.
[34] See Chapter 2: 'The Interrogation of Anna Ardin'.
[35] Ibid.
[36] See Chapter 1: 'The Interrogation of Sofia Wilén'.
[37] A major Swedish tabloid.

INTRODUCTION:
AUGUST HEAT

These are the transcripts of the police interrogations in the case of Julian Assange, which was opened by Anna Ardin and Sofia Wilén on Friday 20 August 2010 in Stockholm, Sweden; along with lab results for two condoms said to have been used during the sexual encounters. The documents in this book form part of the formal submission to the UK courts. The work with the translation, carried out by radsoft.net and rixstep.com, began as soon as the existence and location of the documents became known. The last of the translations went online five days after the discovery. The translations represent well over 30,000 words, and include the interrogations of Anna Ardin, Julian Assange, Sofia Wilén, and nine witnesses, two of whom were acquainted with Julian Assange.

Many of the interrogations were conducted by telephone, and most were not recorded; this despite guidelines that testimony in such cases be *video* recorded. Only the testimonies of those considered supportive of Julian Assange were recorded, and then only as audio recordings. There is also mention of police audio recording equipment breaking down during the course of an interrogation (that of Donald Boström).

When Swedish police create transcripts of recorded police interrogations, every effort is made to bring the reader into the actual interrogation, transcribing every audible sound - every 'er', every 'um', every non-word, every pause. Grammatical mistakes and lapses of continuity are deliberately retained to give the inspectors the precise context in which the interrogations took place, as well as their nuances.

Significantly, while care was taken to be as accurate as possible in the transcription of the audio-recorded interrogations, all interrogations considered to be 'non-supportive' of Julian Assange were 'conceptual' in nature – that is, the interrogators took 'notes' and paraphrased as they saw fit.

The first interrogation was that of Sofia Wilén herself in the late afternoon of Friday 20 August. The interrogation was interrupted when she and the interrogator, Criminal Inspector Irmeli Krans, a close associate of Anna Ardin, were informed that Julian Assange was under arrest in absentia for rape and sexual molestation and that the police were out looking for him on the streets of Stockholm. Sofia Wilén broke down at this point. Criminal Inspector Krans said that there was no way she could continue the interrogation or read Sofia's testimony back to her and get Sofia's formal approval.

The testimony was, however, altered early the next week by Criminal Inspector Krans and her superior, Chief Inspector Mats Gehlin. Criminal Inspector Krans was ordered by Chief Inspector Gehlin to replace the original file with the amended file on 26 August. Criminal Inspector Krans protested against this action, as the police document system 'DurTvå' was specifically designed to prevent wrongdoing. To this day, Sofia's testimony therefore bears an incorrect date —26 August—and not 20 August, which was the actual date when she was interrogated.

The second interrogation was by telephone the following day, Saturday 21 August, to Anna Ardin. In the course of this interrogation, Ardin said that she still *might* have the condom she accused Julian Assange of deliberately breaking (which was notable since the encounter had taken place over a week before).

At 16:48 that same Saturday 21 August 2010, Chief Prosecutor Eva Finné dismissed the rape allegations and formally rescinded the arrest warrant against Julian Assange. Finné had reviewed the uncompleted and unapproved interrogation of Sofia Wilén and concluded that, although she believed Sofia Wilén was telling the truth, no crime had been committed. Chief Prosecutor Finné was later to instruct Chief Inspector Mats Gehlin to regard Sofia Wilén's case as closed and *not* to undertake any actions of his own in its regard—an order Gehlin deliberately violated.

This is coincidentally when Chief Inspector Gehlin decided to send a condom provided as evidence by Sofia Wilén to the state crime lab. As Sofia Wilén's case had been closed by Finné because 'no crime had been committed', Chief Inspector Gehlin had to sneak Wilén's condom to the crime lab by submitting it under Ardin's case number. In addition, approximately one hour after the news broke that the warrant against Julian Assange had been rescinded, the Stockholm police arrived at the residence of Anna Ardin to collect the broken condom Ardin claimed could still be found.

On Monday 30 August, a third interrogation was conducted, this time with Julian Assange. The interrogation was in person and an audio recording was made. This took place in the early evening as Assange's lawyer Leif Silbersky had been in court all day. Curious is the fact that the interpreter used, Gun von Krusenstjerna, was neither formally approved or even qualified for such a task but, on the other hand, did have excellent connections with the US embassy in town.

The next day, Tuesday 1 September, the case regarding the rape allegations was reopened by Director of Public Prosecution Marianne Ny after an appeal by the women's lawyer, Claes Borgström.

The remaining interrogations included here began a week later and were finally concluded on 27 October, 68 days—over two full months—after the allegations were first made on 20 August 2010.

Clearly these documents are of central and crucial relevance to one of the most important legal cases of our times. In addition, the lab report for the two condoms shows that when the Swedish state lab SKL tested Anna Ardin's condom for chromosomal DNA, strikingly, they found none. As chromosomal DNA from both parties inundates condoms during intercourse, the lab result indicates that this condom, although presented as evidence, was never actually used—a matter the Swedish media have kept hidden from their readers for all these years.

As Swedish is not a language that is commonly known in most of the world, it provides a formidable barrier to transparency. We have made the translations of these documents available, so that all may understand the evidence in this case.

A final note: proceeds from the sales of this book will be donated to the Julian Assange Defence Fund.

TRANSLATOR'S NOTE

The truth will out, the truth wins out.

30,000 words in five days. Translators normally manage about 2,000 words per day. This feat was by no means a world record, but it was difficult and a lot of hard work.

The roughest parts were the transcripts. Transcripts are the next best thing to being there—to having a video recording. The task of the transcriber is to record every non-word, sound, and pause in addition to the actual content; this to convey as accurately as possible the attitude and reactions of the interviewee.

Good translations normally never attempt a 'word for word' approach. It's not only words that differ in different languages - it's the ideas and concepts as well. The goal of a translator is to get the idea across, rather than produce stilted language no one really grasps. But the translations of these transcripts necessarily took another approach: to reproduce all the commas, full stops, ellipses, and even the strange constructs exactly as they were found in the originals.

There's only one way to study these documents: as a whole, and with the working assumption that everyone is telling the truth.

The 'case' (if one dare call it that) hovers on two incidents. One takes place in Enköping in the morning. The two people involved have a simple exchange of two lines each before going at it again for what likely is the fifth time in a long sleepless night. The woman has just come back to bed after being out early and shopping, the two of them make love again, and start dozing off to sleep.

Suddenly the one starts all over again. The woman senses the man is about to penetrate her.

> 'What are you wearing?'
> 'I'm wearing you.'
> 'I hope you don't have HIV.'
> 'No of course not.'[1]

And that's it. They weren't well acquainted, the one may have conveyed a desire to always use protection, but it's impossible she would have also conveyed (or spoken outright) about her near phobia about it. Most importantly, the resumption of sex immediately after that simple exchange can in no way indicate to the man that the woman had any objections to continuing—she, in fact, did continue herself.

Perpetration has to assume overriding someone else's wishes. There is nothing at all here approaching that.

The other incident takes place earlier chronologically. It's the story of a very clumsy act of love between a man hard put in a situation where his contract has been broken by the other party, and a woman who really seemed to want to claim a trophy. The girl in question has been described as a lesbian; many of her interests revolve around lesbianism; her friends demonstrated misandry at the crayfish party; certainly any heterosexual activities with this woman would have been strange at the very least.

The 'ado' about being pinned down was obviously a total non-event. As soon as the man noticed the strange behaviour of the woman, he stopped and asked her point blank what she was doing. Aggressors don't do this.

The woman explained she was reaching for a condom. 'OK then' was the man's reply in so many words, and he let her get the condom which was then used for the continuation.

The truth will out, the truth wins out. There is no case here. Which makes it all the more evident another agenda might be at work. The way Investigator Irmeli Krans objected to hunting Assange and calling the incidents 'rape' when no testimony at all had yet been obtained, the fright of Sofia Wilén when she found out what was going on, the way Krans was locked out of the computer database— these all point to something sinister. How can you charge someone with a crime when you don't yet have any data at all to back it up?

And of course it all must inevitably boil down to the classic 'he said/she said' stalemate. Because the first and most sacrosanct rule of jurisprudence is, has always been, and must always remain 'presumption of innocence' together with 'proven beyond a reasonable doubt'. The Swedish courts, under considerable pressure from the rabid Swedish radical feminist lobby, have to rule in cases where no witnesses or forensic evidence can be found. The infamous Thomas Quick cases, some eight in number, where the attorney did nothing for his client for seven years, were based on testimony from the perpetrator himself—a known pathological liar. And yet they're being overturned now anyway, one by one. The cases in August 2010 are not the same at all—they're strictly 'he said/she said', there is no forensic evidence, there is nothing tangible even hinting at a crime, and yet it's pursued anyway. That bad smell isn't from Denmark.

The truth will out, the truth wins out. Let no journalist ever again speculate into what the protocols say. The actual documents are now part of the formal submission to the UK courts.

Yet more: these documents are an indictment of all 'news organisations' who've printed inaccuracies all along or, even worse, refused to print anything at all. Nick Davies' account of the protocols was skewed; both *Aftonbladet* and *Expressen* had copies early on and printed nothing. Some bloggers had copies but arrogantly kept the information to their Sméagol selves.

There'd have been no case and consequently no media hysteria if the truth had come out from the beginning. Tabloids had an interest in only publishing 'juicy details' and not exposing the truth (and thereby killing the entire story). Those opposed to WikiLeaks had similar interests. Keep the truth hidden and the agendas can continue.

That won't work anymore. The documents are here. Good reading.

---

[1] See Chapter 1: The Interrogation of Sofia Wilén.

CHAPTER 1:
THE INTERROGATION OF SOFIA WILÉN

FRIDAY 20 AUGUST 2010

Sofia Wilén and Anna Ardin arrived at the Klara police station in downtown Stockholm on Friday afternoon 20 August 2010. The interrogation of Sofia was conducted by Criminal Inspector Irmeli Krans that same day.

Krans and Wilén were informed during the interrogation that Julian Assange had been arrested in absentia and that the police were hunting for him in the Stureplan nightclub area.

Krans, an acquaintance of Anna Ardin, noted that Wilén seemed to go to pieces on hearing the news and that she therefore decided to abort the interrogation without the protocol being read back to her or approved by her.

After the complaints against Julian were dismissed, Criminal Inspector Krans and her superior Chief Inspector Mats Gehlin attempted to alter Sofia's testimony, something not only forbidden by police regulations, but also technically impossible to achieve—for good reason—with the 'DurTvå' document system in use. As attempts to overwrite the conflicting first version from 20 August proved unsuccessful, Criminal Inspector Krans created and signed a new interrogation on 26 August. The correspondence between Criminal Inspector Krans, Chief Inspector Gehlin, and Eva Finné regarding these changes is provided below.

Criminal Inspector Krans was thereafter taken off the case, but the version presented to Assange's legal counsel was the amended version from 26 August and not the original from 20 August. It cannot be adequately stressed that if Sofia Wilén never had her original testimony read back to her and never approved it either, then that certainly holds double for the version Criminal Inspector Krans and Chief Inspector Gehlin inserted into the system six days later.

Krans wrote on 1 September as follows.

> *Friday 20 August 2010: I conducted an interrogation with Sofia Wilén in the case 0201-K246314-10 at the Klara police station. The interrogation began at 16:21 and was concluded before being completed or reviewed or approved at 18:40. It was logged into the word processing application DurTvå. The interrogation was to be copyedited the next work day, Monday 23 August 2010. This was not possible because I was denied access to the interrogation I'd conducted. After a*

few message exchanges I was given the directive by officer Mats Gehlin to instead create and sign a new interrogation in DurTvå which was carried out 26 August with the necessary modifications. Unfortunately that document was dated and time stamped with the date and time of the correction automatically by the DurTvå system.

The interrogation is in the loosest possible form, a so-called 'conceptual interrogation' ('konceptförhör'). The interrogation therefore takes the form of a narrative.

Signed by:	Irmeli Krans
Police authority:	Stockholm municipality
Date signed:	2010-08-26 15:04
Unit:	1/NJ On duty section
Journal #:	0201-K246336-10
Interrogated:	Wilén, Sofia
The interrogated is:	Complainant
Civil registration #:	
Identify confirmed:	No
Relation to the suspect - complainant - witness:	
Interpreter:	
Language:	
Suspected crime / reason for interrogation:	Because of suspected rape Tuesday 17 August 2010
Advised of suspicion:	
Advised of right to attorney:	
Defender/representative is desired:	
Defender/representative is present:	
Accepts defender provided by the court:	
Chief interrogator:	Irmeli Krans
Date:	2010-08-26
Interrogation commenced:	14:43
Interrogation concluded:	18:40
Place of interrogation:	Klara local police station
Type of interrogation:	RB 23:6[1]
Method of interrogation:	
Interrogation witness:	
Transcribed by:	

Sofia says she saw an interview a few weeks ago on TV with Julian Assange who is known to be behind the WikiLeaks publication of US military documents from Afghanistan. Sofia thought he was interesting, courageous, and admirable. For the next two weeks she watched the news carefully, she read a lot of articles, and saw interviews. One evening when she sat at home and Googled the name Julian Assange she discovered he was invited to Sweden to hold a lecture arranged by the social democrat Brotherhood movement. She posted a message to the Brotherhood press secretary Anna Ardin whose contact details she found on their website and asked if he would be coming to Sweden and if she in such case could attend his lecture. She offered to help out with practical details in return. Anna Ardin replied that she'd forward her message to those in charge.

But Sofia got no further reply and suddenly one day she saw an ad with the time and place for the lecture. The lecture was to be held in 'LO-borgen' at Norra Bantorget Saturday 14 August. She rang those in charge on Friday and asked if it was OK to attend. She was told she was one of the first to apply and it'd be OK. She took the day off from work and went to LO-borgen on Saturday. She saw a woman who she presumed was Anna Ardin standing outside LO-borgen and went up to her and introduced herself. Anna told Sofia that she was on the list so she was welcome to attend. At the same time the lecturer himself, Julian Assange, approached with a man in his 30s. She got the impression the man was Julian's press secretary or something similar. Julian looked at Sofia as if he was amused. She got the feeling he thought she didn't belong there in her shocking pink cashmere jumper amongst all the other grey journalists.

THE LECTURE

She sat at the far right front when she entered the venue, the lecturer would stand all the way to the left. The room seemed full of journalists. A half hour before the lecture was to begin, Anna approached Sofia and asked if she could help buy a cable for Julian's computer. They needed a cable and Sofia had offered to help out. Sofia went up to Julian to ask what type of cable he needed. He explained what he needed and then wrote it down on a small piece of paper. She took the paper and placed it immediately in her pocket. Julian looked contemptibly at her and said 'you didn't even look at the note'. She told him she didn't need to as he'd already explained what type of cable he needed.

She took a cab to the 'Webhallen' boutique on Sveavägen but they were closed. The time was 10:30 and the store would open first at 11:00. But that's also when the lecture was scheduled to begin, so Sofia started feeling stressed. The cabbie drove her instead to the Haymarket where she purchased two types of cable for safety's sake. She got back in time, she had the right type of cable, but she wasn't thanked for her help by Julian. The lecture went well.

THE LUNCH

There were many journalists who wanted to interview Julian after the lecture. Sofia stayed around because she too wanted to speak with him. She asked Anna if this was possible and Anna said Julian would stand outside the entrance to LO-borgen to be accessible to the public in case anyone wanted to ask him questions. Sofia went out and sat in the shade and waited for the interviews to be over. There were more interviews outside. Sofia approached LO-borgen again and overheard that the Brotherhood people were going to treat Julian to lunch. Sofia asked if she could come along too, after all she'd helped them with the cable. She was invited and went together with Anna, Julian and his entourage, and two members of the Brotherhood to a restaurant on Drottninggatan across from the Central Bathhouse. She ended up next to Julian and started talking with him. He looked at her now and again during the lunch. On one occasion when he put cheese on his *knäckebröd* she asked him if it tasted good and then he reached over with his sandwich and fed her with it. Later during lunch he said he needed a charger for his laptop. She said she could get one for him, after all she'd got the cable for him earlier. He put his arm around her and said 'yes you gave me the cable'. Sofia thought this was flattering for it was obvious he was now flirting with her.

The others left after lunch, leaving only Sofia, Julian, and Julian's companion. They went off together to buy an electric cable for

Julian's computer. 'Kjell & Co' didn't have the product, so they went on to Webhallen but it was closed again. They walked back on Sveavägen towards the Haymarket and talked about what they'd do next. Julian's companion asked him if he wanted to come along and help move furniture for his parents and Sofia offered Julian a visit at the natural history museum where she worked. It was decided Julian would accompany Sofia to the museum and his companion left them. Julian and Sofia went into the Haymarket subway station where she purchased a blue access card good for the day as he didn't have the monthly commuter card and no money either as he said. They took the train towards *Mörby Centrum* and stepped off at the university stop. A man in the subway recognised Julian and told him how much he admired him.

THE NATURAL HISTORY MUSEUM

On the way from the university subway station Julian stopped to pet a few dogs, which Sofia thought was charming. In the museum they went to the staff room where Julian sat down and starting surfing the net, he was looking for tweets about himself. They sat there waiting for a film that was to be shown at Cosmonova at 18:00.

They were let into the cinema by Sofia's colleague and Julian held Sofia's hand. In the darkness of the cinema he started kissing her. A few latecomers arrived and sat behind them and so they moved to a row at the back. Julian continued kissing her, touched her breasts under her jumper, undid her bra, unbuttoned her pants, caressed her buttocks, and sucked her nipples. He muttered about the armrest being in the way. She was sitting in his lap when the lights went on and he tried to put her bra back on. She thought it embarrassing to sit there in view of her colleagues who she knew could have seen it all.

They went out through the inner courtyard and she went to the toilet. When she came out, he was lying on his back on a picnic table resting, he said he was very tired. He was supposed to be at a crayfish party at 20:00 and wanted to sleep 20 minutes before leaving. They lay down together in the grass next to each other and he had his arm around her. He fell asleep and she woke him twenty minutes later.

Then they promenaded over lawns, passed cows and Canadian geese, he held her hand, it was wonderful in all possible ways and he told her 'you're very attractive to me'. He'd also told her in the cinema she had pretty breasts. She asked him if they'd meet again. He said of course they would, they'd meet after the crayfish party.

She accompanied him to the Zinkensdamm subway station where he caught a cab back to Anna Ardin's where the party was to take place. He gave her a hug and said he didn't want to part from her and encouraged her to charge her cell phone. She went home to Enköping, arriving at home at 23:00. She had a voice message waiting from Julian from 22:55 when she'd recharged her phone, telling her to ring him when her phone was working again. She rang back at 23:15, realising he was still at the party. She'd developed a stomach cramp from a sandwich she'd eaten on the way home and told him she wanted to go to bed. He insinuated it wasn't about stomach cramps as much as a feeling of guilt.

ON MONDAY

She rang Julian twice on Sunday but his phone was turned off. She told her colleagues at work on Monday what had happened at the weekend. They told her Julian felt dumped and therefore hadn't rung back so that the ball was in her court. She rang him and he answered. She asked if they should do something together. He said he'd be at a meeting which could take a long time up until 20:30 but he could ring her back later. He also asked about her stomach cramps. He insinuated she'd lied about her cramps and he used the third person to tell her. She promised to wait for him so after she finished work at 19:00 she went to *Kungshallarna* and had sushi. Afterwards she strolled about town and ended up in the old town where she rang him back at 21:00 when he still hadn't got back to her, asking what was going on. He said he was in a meeting in Hornsgatan and he wanted her to come there. She got the address and went there. She couldn't find the address when she arrived, rang Julian, and spoke with a man who spoke Swedish who explained she was to get in through a side entrance. She stood there and waited for him when he came out together with another man, they said goodbye to one another and looked very happy.

Julian and Sofia walked up Hornsgatan towards Slussen and from there to the old town. They sat by the water at Munkbroleden and he commented on girls who sat there as 'lonely and abandoned' and who 'probably need saving'. They lay down and starting making out, heavily. Amongst other things he put his hands under her jumper and when they left the area she noticed people were looking at them. They decided to go home to her place. They went into the subway where his card was now invalid and she got him through by swiping her own card twice. They took the train to Enköping from the central station, she paid for the tickets, SEK 107 (~$10) each. He claimed he didn't want to use his credit card, he didn't want to be traced. They sat in the direction the train would move all the way back in the car. Julian connected his computer and started reading about himself on Twitter on the computer and on the phone. He devoted more attention to the computer than he did to her. She'd suggested they take in at a hotel but he said he wanted to see 'girls in their natural habitat'.

TO ENKÖPING

It was dark when they got off the train and they passed old industry buildings where he went off to pee. She also took a pee. When they arrived at her flat she went in before him into the bedroom to clean up a bit before he saw it. They took off their shoes and the relationship between them didn't feel warm anymore. The passion and excitement had disappeared. They made out in the bedroom but she wanted to brush her teeth. It was midnight, pitch black outside, and they brushed their teeth together—it felt banal and boring.

When they want back in the bedroom Julian stood in front of Sofia and grabbed her hips and pushed her demonstratively down on the bed, as if he were a real man. He took off his clothes and they had foreplay on the bed. They were naked and he rubbed his penis against her nether regions without penetrating her but he got closer and closer to her slit. She squeezed her legs together because she didn't want sex with him without protection. They carried on for hours and Julian couldn't get a full erection. Julian had no interest in using a condom.

Suddenly Julian said he was going to go to sleep. She felt rejected and shocked. It came so suddenly, they'd had a really long foreplay and then nothing. She asked what was wrong, she didn't understand. He pulled the blanket over himself, turned away from her, and fell asleep. She went out and got her fleece blanket because she was cold. She lay awake a long time wondering what had happened and exchanged SMS messages with her friends. He lay beside her snoring. She must have fallen asleep for later she woke up and they had sex. She'd earlier got the condoms and put them on the floor by the bed. He reluctantly agreed to use a condom even if he muttered something about preferring her to latex. He no longer had an erection problem. At one point when he mounted her from behind, she turned to look at him and smiled and he asked her why she was smiling, what she had to smile about. She didn't like the tone in his voice.

They fell asleep and when they woke up they could have had sex again, she's not really sure. He ordered her to get water and orange juice. She didn't like being ordered in her own home but thought 'whatever' and got the water and juice anyway. He wanted her to go out and buy more breakfast. She didn't want to leave him alone in the flat, she didn't know him well enough, but she did it anyway. When she left the flat he lay naked in her bed and was working with his phones. Before she left she said 'be good'. He replied 'don't worry, I'm always bad'. When she returned she served him oatmeal, milk, and juice. She'd already eaten before he woke up and spoken with a friend on the phone.

THE ASSAULT

They sat on the bed and talked and he took off her clothes again. They had sex again and she discovered he'd put the condom only over the head of his penis but she let it be. They fell asleep and she woke by feeling him penetrate her. She immediately asked 'are you wearing anything' and he answered 'you'. She told him 'you better not have HIV' and he replied 'of course not'. She felt it was too late. He was already inside her and she let him continue. She couldn't be bothered telling him again. She'd been nagging about condoms all night long. She's never had unprotected sex. He said he wanted to

23

come inside her, he didn't say when he'd done it but he did it. There was a lot running out of her afterwards.

She told him what happens if she gets pregnant. He replied that Sweden was a good country for raising children. She told him jokingly that if she got pregnant then he'd have to pay her student loans. On the train to Enköping he'd told her he'd slept in Anna Ardin's bed after the crayfish party. She asked if he'd had sex with Anna but he said Anna liked girls, she was lesbian. But now she knows he did the same thing with Anna. She asked him how many times he'd had sex but he said he hadn't counted. He also said he'd had a HIV test three months earlier and he'd had sex with a girl afterwards and that girl had also taken a HIV test and wasn't infected. She said sarcastic things to him in a joking tone. She thinks she got the idea of taking the drama out of what had happened, he in turn didn't seem to care. When he found out how big her student loan was he said if he paid her so much money she'd have to give birth to the baby. They joked that they'd name the baby Afghanistan. He also said that he should always carry abortion pills that actually were sugar pills.

His phone rang and he had a meeting with *Aftonbladet* on Tuesday at noon. She explained to him that he'd not make the meeting on time and he pushed his entire schedule forward an hour. Then they rode her bicycle to the train station. She paid his ticket to Stockholm. Before they parted he told her to keep her phone on. She asked if he'd ring her and he said he would.

AFTERWARDS

She rode her bicycle home, showered, and washed her bed sheets. Because she hadn't made it to work she called in sick and stayed home the whole day. She wanted to clean up and wash everything. There was semen on the bed sheets, she thought it was disgusting. She went to the chemist's and bought a 'morning after' pill.

When she talked with her friends afterwards she understood she was the victim of a crime. She went into Danderyd hospital and went from there to the *Söder* hospital. There she was examined and they even took samples with a so-called 'rape kit'.

FORENSIC CERTIFICATE

Sofia gives her permission for obtaining a forensic certificate.

COUNSEL FOR THE CLAIMANT

Sofia desires a counsel for the claimant she will identify later.

SUNDRY

Julian says his name is Julian Paul Assange and was born 31 December 1971.

INTERROGATOR'S COMMENTS [CRIMINAL INSPECTOR KRANS]

Sofia and I were notified during the interrogation that Julian Assange had been arrested in absentia. Sofia had difficulty concentrating after that news, whereby I made the judgement it was best to terminate the interrogation. But Sofia had time anyway to explain that Assange was angry with her. I didn't have time to get any further details about why he was angry with her or how this manifested itself. And we didn't have time to get into what else happened afterwards. The interrogation was neither read back to Sofia nor reviewed for approval by her but Sofia was told she had the opportunity to do this later.

THE ORIGINAL INTERROGATION

Interrogator Irmeli Krans had difficulty transcribing her incomplete interrogation with Sofia. She was denied access by her superior Mats Gehlin. Following is correspondence between her (IK), Gehlin (MG) and Eva Finné (EF) in that regard.

2010-08-23 08:27 IK to MG
Hi, I hope I've done it right now and the document will get to you as

it should. Please send an acknowledgement. About the verbal presentation for the prosecutor, I have no further information other than what's already been done by telephone by Linda Wassgren at some time during the interrogation. I don't know what was presented as Wassgren doesn't want to communicate with me. An opportunity to classify the crime with the prosecutor was not given me but I was told it would be classified as rape according to a directive by the prosecutor. Greetings, Irmeli Krans

2010-08-24 09:33 MG to IK
Do like this. Paste this into your interrogation and sign it. It'd look funny if I signed it. I'm attaching the old interrogation.

2010-08-24 13:38 IK to MG
Hi, I might be thick but I don't really understand what you mean. Anders Ringkvist is trying to help me and we've tried contacting you without being able to resolve the issue.

2010-08-24 13:44 MG to IK
Create a new interrogation. Paste in the text and address the interrogation to the case. And sign the interrogation.

2010-08-24 16:35 IK to MG
OK but then there'll be two interrogations. But there's only been one formal interrogation, by me at any rate. Where does the other interrogation disappear to? If it's to be done right then I assume I have to make modifications in the original interrogation and sign it. With the risk of appearing difficult I do not want to have an unsigned document with my name circulating in DurTvå space. Particularly not now when the case has developed as it has.

2010-08-30 09:32 MG to EF
The case ...
(Rest deleted - the subject line is 'The Case' (Ärendet). The body text was removed by the judicial authority at the behest of the chief prosecutor.)

2010-08-30 09:33 EF to MG
The complaint about molestation isn't here.

2010-08-30 09:35 MG to EF
OK I thought you wanted the case that had been dismissed. Delete what you received and you'll get a new one.

---

[1] See http://lawline.se/answers/3119.

CHAPTER 2:
THE INTERROGATION OF ANNA ARDIN
SATURDAY 21 AUGUST 2010

THE INTERROGATION OF ANNA ARDIN

The interrogation of Anna Ardin took place by telephone the day after Sofia Wilén's —21 August—a matter of hours before Chief Prosecutor Eva Finné would dismiss most of the complaints against Julian Assange and rescind the arrest warrant that had caused the worldwide media stir.

The chief interrogator was Sara Wennerblom. The interrogation began at 11:31 and was concluded at 12:20—forty nine minutes.

Anna Ardin tells Sara Wennerblom in the course of this interview that she probably has the condom lying around (editor's note: she still had the condom even though it was several days after the encounter?) but never checked if it was broken—this despite her supposedly being so worried that she went to the police.

As for Sofia Wilén, this interrogation is a 'conceptual interrogation' ('konceptförhör'), which takes the form of a narrative.

Signed by:	
Police authority:	Stockholm municipality
Date signed:	2010-08-26 15:04
Unit:	1/NJ On duty section
Journal #:	0201-K246336-10
Interrogated:	Ardin, Anna
The interrogated is:	Complainant
Civil registration #:	
Identify confirmed:	No
Relation to the suspect - complainant - witness:	
Interpreter:	
Language:	
Suspected crime / reason for interrogation:	Rape or sexual molestation at Tjurbergsgatan 36 up to 2010-08-14 12:00
Advised of suspicion:	
Advised of right to attorney:	
Defender/representative is desired:	
Defender/representative is present:	
Accepts defender provided by the court:	
Chief interrogator:	Sara Wennerblom
Date:	2010-08-21
Interrogation commenced:	11:31
Interrogation concluded:	12:20
Place of interrogation:	Klara local police station
Type of interrogation:	RB 23:6[1]
Method of interrogation:	Telephone
Interrogation witness:	
Transcribed by:	

The chief interrogator rings complainant Anna Ardin (hereafter 'Anna') for the purpose of conducting an interrogation because of the event described above ('rape or sexual molestation at Tjurbergsgatan 36 up to 2010-08-14 12:00').

Anna says she's worked as a press secretary and political secretary for Sweden's christian social democrats - the Brotherhood movement. Anna says she was involved in organising a seminar that was to take place on 14 August where Julian Assange had been invited in as a lecturer.

Because Anna would be out of town 11–14 August she lent her flat to Assange. But Anna returned to Stockholm already Friday 13 August because she had a lot of work to do for the seminar. Anna and Assange have never before met personally but only had contact via mail and the telephone.

The Friday in question Assange and Anna went out and ate dinner together. They'd agreed that Assange would go on living in Anna's flat despite her coming home a day early. After their dinner on the town they went back to Anna's flat and drank tea.

In answer to a question Anna says that neither she nor Assange drank alcohol that evening. When they sat and drank tea Assange began caressing her leg. In answer to a question Anna says Assange earlier in the evening had not made any physical approaches save now which Anna initially welcomed. But it felt 'uncomfortable from the get-go' as Assange was rough and impatient. According to Anna, 'everything happened so fast'. He ripped off her clothes and in conjunction with this pulled at and broke her necklace. Anna tried to put some clothes back on again because things were going too fast and it felt uncomfortable but Assange immediately took her clothes off again. Anna says that she thought she actually didn't want to go any further but it was too late to say 'stop' to Assange when she'd 'gone along with it this far'. She thought she 'could blame herself'. So she let Assange fully undress her.

Then they lay in the bed. Anna was on her back and Assange was on top of her. Anna thought Assange wanted to immediately put his penis in her vagina which she didn't want as he didn't have a condom on. So she tried to twist her hips to the side and squeeze her legs together to prevent a penetration. Anna tried several times to reach for a condom which Assange stopped her from doing by holding her arms and prying open her legs and trying nevertheless to penetrate her with his penis without a condom. Anna says that in the end she was ready to cry because she was pinned and couldn't reach a condom and thought 'this might not end well'. In answer to a question Anna says Assange must have known she was trying to reach for a condom and he was holding her arms to stop her.

Assange asked after a while what Anna was doing and why she was squeezing her legs together. Anna then told him she wanted him to put on a condom before he entered her. Assange released her arms and put on the condom Anna got for him. Anna felt a huge unexpressed reluctance from Assange to using a condom which led to her getting the feeling he didn't put on the condom she'd given him. She therefore reached down with her hand to Assange's penis to check if he'd really put the condom on. She could feel that the edge of the condom was where it should be at the root of Assange's penis. Anna and Assange resumed having sex and Anna says she thought 'hope it's over soon'.

Anna notices after a while that Assange withdraws from her to fix the condom. Judging from the sound, it sounded to Anna like Assange took the condom off. He entered her again and continued the act. Anna again checked his penis with her hand and again felt the edge of the condom where it should be and so let the sex continue.

After a while Assange ejaculates inside her and thereafter withdraws. Anna saw that the condom didn't have semen in it when Assange took it off. When Anna began moving her body she noticed how things were running out of her vagina. Anna understood rather quickly that it must be Assange's semen. She pointed this out for Assange but he denied this and told her it was she who was wet with her own juices. Anna is convinced that Assange, when he withdrew from her the first time, deliberately broke the condom at the tip and thereafter continued the sex with the resulting ejaculation. In answer

34

to a question Anna says she didn't look closer at the condom, if it was broken as she thought, but she says she thinks she still has the condom at home and will look at it. She says that even the bed sheets used on that occasion are most likely still in her hamper.

After the above mentioned incident Anna says she and Assange didn't have any more sex. Yet Assange went on living with her up to and including Friday 20 August. According to Anna Assange made sexual overtures every day after that evening when they'd had sex. For example by touching her breasts. Anna rebuffed Assange on all these occasions and Assange accepted it. On one occasion, Wednesday 18 August, he'd suddenly removed all his clothing on his lower body and thereafter rubbed his lower body and his erect penis against Anna. Anna says she thought this was strange behaviour and uncomfortable and had therefore moved down to a mattress on the floor and slept there instead of up in the bed with Assange. The next night Anna stayed with a friend because she didn't want to be around Assange because of his strange behaviour. She even pointed out after Wednesday 18 August that she didn't want Assange staying any longer in her flat which he didn't respond to until Friday when he took his things and returned her flat key.

In answer to a question Anna says Assange lived with her but they hardly slept together because Assange was up at night working with his computer. She mostly got up in the morning about 07:00 when he went to sleep.

In answer to a question Anna says she knew of Sofia when she'd been in contact with Anna before the above mentioned seminar and been part of the audience. According to Anna Sofia had purchased electrical cables for Assange and been with Anna and Assange at the lunch after the seminar. Anna noticed Assange flirted with Sofia during the lunch and understood that they'd afterwards begun some sort of relationship when Assange rang Sofia later in the evening when he was at Anna's at the crayfish party.

She received an email message from Sofia Friday 20 August where she wonders if she can reach Assange as she had something important to tell him. Anna understood immediately what it was about and contacted Sofia who then told her what had happened to her, that she and Assange had had sex and that he didn't want to use a condom etc. Sofia wanted to follow this up with the police and Anna decided to follow along, foremost as support.

Anna says she already heard from several sources that Assange 'chases all women who cross his path'. Considering Assange's reputation Anna felt it very important that they used a condom the time they had sex, that is the day before the seminar.

Anna says she's felt terrible after the occasion when she and Assange had sex. Foremost because of the worry she'd been infected by HIV or some other STD. Anna says she freely consented to have sex with Assange but she couldn't have let it happen if she'd known he didn't have a condom. Anna has been in contact with the health centre and been given a time for tests next week. Anna approves of the police having the results of these tests.

Anna does not want any help from the crime victims unit but will get back to us if she feels it's necessary.

Interrogation read back and approved.

---

[1] See http://lawline.se/answers/3119.

CHAPTER 3:
THE INTERROGATION OF JULIAN ASSANGE

MONDAY 30 AUGUST 2010

Julian Assange was questioned a single time by the Swedish police on 30 August 2010. By this time all complaints saved one ('molestation') had been dismissed by Chief Prosecutor Eva Finné.

The interrogation took place late in the day because Assange's legal counsel Leif Silbersky was in court with another trial.

The interrogation lasted 54 minutes with a short pause in the middle to clear up questions Assange wanted to ask the police, specifically related to his apprehension the entire conversation would once again make its way to the tabloid Expressen.

The interrogation took place at the 'family violence' unit of the police at Bergsgatan 48 in Stockholm, began at 17:43, and concluded at 18:37. There were five people present.

> *Mats Gehlin (MG) - the chief interrogator*
> *Ewa Olofsson (EO) - the police interrogation witness*
> *Gun von Krusenstjerna (GK) - the interpreter*
> *Leif Silbersky (LS) - Julian's legal counsel at the time*
> *Julian Assange (JA)*

Leif Silbersky spoke English with his client save on one occasion. Julian Assange's testimony was later translated and transcribed by Jennie Wolgast.

It is important to note that, because the interrogation was conducted in English and subsequently translated into Swedish for the police report, that the English words used in this 'translation of a translation' are not necessarily the words Assange would actually have used at the time. (To see the effect back-translating can have on the original text, try typing a sentence into Google Translate and then translate back and forth between English and your chosen language.) In addition, it is notable that the interpreter used for the interrogation, Gun von Krusenstjerna, who had close ties with the US embassy in Stockholm, was later found to have not been qualified for the assignment.

In contrast to the interrogations for Sofia Wilén and Anna Ardin, which were 'conceptual interrogations', loosely transcribed in narrative form, and despite guidelines that testimony in these cases be video recorded, this interrogation was audio-recorded and subsequently transcribed.

Interestingly, the version of this interrogation submitted to the British courts contained notes made by Assange's Swedish attorney, Björn Hurtig, including passages in the transcript that had been highlighted by him. We have indicated these passages in bold.

Signed by:	Mats Gehlin
Police authority:	Stockholm municipality
Date signed:	2010-08-31 16:42
Unit:	1KU/F Domestic violence group
Journal #:	0201-K246336-10
Interrogated:	Assange, Julien [*sic*] 19710703
The interrogated is:	Suspect
Civil registration #:	
Identify confirmed:	No
Interpreter:	
Language:	
Suspected crime:	Assange is suspected of molestation as follows. Assange has during the time 13-14 August 2010 in the residence of Anna Ardin in Tjurbergsgatan in Stockholm molested Anna Ardin by, during intercourse which was commenced and carried out under the explicit condition that a condom should be used, deliberately destroyed the condom and continued the intercourse until he ejaculated in her vagina.
Advised of suspicion:	Yes
Advised of right to attorney:	Yes
Defender/representative is desired:	
Defender/representative is present:	Yes
Accepts defender provided by the court	
Chief interrogator:	Mats Gehlin
Date:	2010-08-30
Interrogation commenced:	17:43
Interrogation concluded:	18:37
Place of interrogation:	Bergsgatan 48, Domestic violence group
Type of interrogation:	RB 23:6[1]
Method of interrogation:	Audio tape interrogation
Interrogation witness:	
Transcribed by:	

Commentary on transcribed interrogation, case K246376-10, interrogation date 2010-08-30:

Some passages have, at the time of transcription, been translated from English to Swedish and been included in the interrogation because translation by the interpreter did not occur.

Otherwise the interrogation is transcribed according to the interpreter's translation.

2010-08-31

Jennie Wolgast

MG: And now we're running the tape, this will be transcribed, so all parts will be transcribed, in other words the entire interrogation every word will be transcribed.

JA: I have a question.

MG: Wait. And as stated, you are under suspicion and are to be formally notified of this and this is for the crime of **molestation**. And the notification is as follows: Assange has between 13 and 14 August 2010 in Anna Ardin's residence at Tjurbergsgatan in Stockholm molested Anna Ardin by during sex, which was initiated and completed with the explicit condition a condom would be used, with **malice aforethought destroyed the condom** and continued the sex until he ejaculated in her vagina.

LS: And that's it?

MG: Yes.

JA: Is this one or two incidents?

MG: One incident.

JA: The 13th, the 14th...

GK: In the evening or?

MG: It's during the time between the 13th ...

JA: Between, OK.

MG: And so the question, what is your response to this accusation?

LS: Is it correct or not correct?

JA: I'm trying to understand exactly what he said.

GK: You want to repeat it one more time?

MG: I can try to do it too, Assange has during the time the 13th, in other words the time is clear for that matter you know that. The molestation is that you destroyed the condom.

JA. OK.

MG: And that you did this with malice aforethought.

JA: So in other words there are several condoms?

MG: Yes in this context, no in this context this is about one condom on one occasion.

JA: OK, so it's one incident ...

GK: One condom.

JA: ... Between the 13th and the 14th when I, when, you say I have deliberately destroyed a condom during sex.

LS: Correct. What is your response to that?

JA: It's not true.

MG: OK, so that you can then tell us your experience of the evening in question, is it true that you and Anna were out eating dinner?

JA: What date?

MG: The 13th.

JA: What day of the week is that?

LS: I can check, or tell you. The 13th of August was a Friday.

MG: And then the question, were you aware of, if one expresses it like that, were you aware of an event where you had sex together?

JA: Before I answer that, can I assume that this is going to end up in *Expressen*?

MG: From us? I'm not going to leak anything. And the only thing that's here, that's the three of us who are a part of this interrogation and a girl who will transcribe it afterwards. And I'm the only one who has access to the file. So if it gets into *Expressen*, you can pick a fight with me.

JA: And if the case continues?

MG: Yes after this interrogation the prosecutor will decide whether to continue or close the case.

JA: Previous statements, all the previous statements.

MG: From?

JA: From this office.

MG: It's gone out through a reviewer. And that is, who censors things about the investigation.
JA: So it'll be the same thing here what I say then?

MG: Yes but this ... Yes one can say the secrecy act says nothing will be released about what's happened. No individuals will be outed. So that this occurs for each document, someone sits down and blackens whatever isn't supposed to come out. But we have the law that things have to be checked for confidentiality and whatever isn't censored by law, we're forced to release.

JA: So this part of the conversation, as an example, will be released?

MG: Your questions about it, if it's nothing except for you.

JA: And who decides that?

MG: That's our legal department.

LS: I think you should respond, because if they accuse you of something you haven't responded to, they have to accept what the girl says. You have to defend yourself by telling them your version. For otherwise it will become known you didn't respond and then the prosecutor has to go to court with it.

JA: OK.

LS: But if you respond then the court, the prosecutor, get your version and the girl's version then the prosecutor has to decide 'can I prove he's done this'.

JA: And how much of my version do I have to tell?

MG: One more thing, you have the right during the interrogation to take a break from the interrogation. And then we turn off the tape and if you don't want to have this discussion we're having now, because the interrogation is actually only supposed to be about the alleged crime.

LS: It's even easier than that, if I can take it in Swedish, it's even easier than that, you can translate. Either you destroyed the condom deliberately as the girl says or so it's an accident or so there's been no condom used whatsoever. Those are the possible alternatives. So submit your alternative to the police.

JA: All I'm saying ...

MG: Do you want us to take a break so we can finish discussing this so you feel calmer about things?

LS: Do you want a discussion ...

JA: Maybe we should have a discussion.

LS: OK we'll take a break.

MG: We pause for clarifications about the interrogation and the time is 17:55.

MG: The interrogation is resumed at 18:02. And if I put it like this, you denied the crime and so I ask, are you aware of an event where a condom broke during sex with Anna?

JA: No.

MG: Have you had ...

JA: I ... I've heard the accusation.

MG: You've heard the accusation. From whom?

JA. Friday the 20th August. The same day the police were contacted I spoke with Anna and Anna accused me of a lot of things. And there were a number of false statements as well. During the conversation she made a similar accusation, she said that I'd removed the condom during sex. The first time I heard the accusation.

MG: Is it true you've had a sexual relationship, you and Anna?

JA: Yes we had a sexual relationship from the, Friday the 13th, a couple of days. We slept in the same bed until the following Friday.

MG: So how was this sexual relationship, were there multiple occasions?

JA: Yes.

MG: Was a condom used on any of these occasions?

JA: On the first occasion. And we had sex several times on the 13th and the 14th. And afterwards, on the other days too, we also had a sexual relationship.

MG: So, the later sexual relations, so it was intercourse?

JA: No they were more we touched each other.

MG: So that, we're talking about one time it's about intercourse?

JA: Yes we had intercourse the 13th and the 14th.

MG: And that was once or was it multiple times?

JA: Multiple times.

MG: **And you used a condom the first time?**

JA: Yes.

MG: And who wanted to use a condom?

JA: I'm not certain.

MG: And why wasn't a condom used for the other sex acts?

JA: It was used for the other sex acts.

MG: OK I misunderstood. **So you had sex only with a condom?**

JA: **Yes that's correct.**

MG: The accusation is the condom, a condom, was damaged after the act and Anna is of the opinion that at one point when you withdraw your penis there was a sound like you first removed the condom but when you entered her again she reached down and felt and she could feel you still had the condom on. Then you ejaculated and she feels amongst other things that she has semen in her. And she looks at the condom and there's no semen in the condom. And so the question to you, is this a situation you recognise in any way?

JA: No. At one point Anna pointed to the bed which had a wet spot. And said, look at that. And said, is that you? I said, no it has to be you. And we didn't talk about it anymore, at all, not at all. Until the accusations on Friday, a week later.

MG: And we're talking about the first occasion again ...

JA: And during this time, except one night Anna and I slept in the same bed. Every night except Tuesday and Thursday nights. On Thursday evening Anna said she was going out a few hours to visit with a journalist who wrote something about me who lived in the same area or the same building or close by. But she didn't return that evening.

MG: Do you remember what you did with the condom?

JA: No.

MG: And you have no recollection of a damaged condom?

JA: No. And I've not looked around for a damaged condom.

MG: Do you use a condom otherwise?

JA: Yes usually, not always but usually.

MG: And you say you didn't check, or you say you don't remember what you did with the condom, is that correct?

JA: Yes that is correct.

MG: Normally how do you do things?

JA: I have no special routines for what I do with condoms.

MG: No. How did you become acquainted with Anna?

JA: When I now think back to that situation, it wasn't an unusual situation for me and I had no reason to suspect I'd be accused of something afterwards. No it wasn't a question of any accusations whatsoever in any way so I don't really remember when I heard the first accusation before Friday. So I didn't recollect that evening and the night in greater detail.

MG: No.

JA: You asked how I got to know Anna. To get here to Sweden it was necessary for me to get diplomatic support to leave England. Because of my security situation between my organisation and the Pentagon. Political contacts in Sweden therefore suggested I should be invited by the christian democrats to hold a speech and a formal invitation would be sent to England, so that I would get a secure transit here. From England. And I understood Anna Ardin was press secretary for the Brotherhood movement within the christian democrats.

MG: A correction, it's not the christian democrats but the social democrats.

GK: Sorry, sorry, I apologise for naming the wrong political party.

MG: Yes.

GK: Forgive me, excuse me. The social democrats.

JA: She was contacted by Peter. I don't remember his surname. I think he's the chairman of the Brotherhood, and a good man. Anna offered her flat to me. Was also involved in the arranging of the press conference last Friday, on Friday.

MG: And when did you arrive in Sweden?

JA: Wednesday or Thursday.

MG: And the date?

JA: I'm not certain. Maybe the 12th. Between the 10th and the 12th.

MG: This accusation, I might sound like a nag but I still have to ask. It's a rather clear picture Anna has of what happened. And this part of her hearing a sound from the condom.

JA: Anna Ardin has never spoken to me about this incident in any way. Or anyone else I'm aware of. I received a very brief and completely different reference, something other than what you're saying now, on Friday the 20th.

MG: What do you think Anna meant by pointing to the wet spot?

JA: I had no idea at the time. She might have been trying to point out how loving the sex had been.

MG: But she said something about it coming from you.

JA: Yes she said was it from you or?

MG: Why did she do that if you had a condom?

JA: I don't know that.

MG: Did you check the condom beforehand?

JA: Before what?

MG: Before you put the condom on, so to speak.

JA: No, I don't make a habit of checking them in detail before I put them on. There was nothing unusual there in any way. So I didn't inspect the condom in any special way. And I didn't ignore it completely either.

MG: Who put the condom on?

JA: I can't remember.

MG: You don't remember who took it off either?

JA: It was mostly likely me. It's unusual with women removing condoms.

MG: Then you said you had sex, did you have more sex that evening?

JA: We took several pauses and then began again, with the same condom.

MG: So this was an extended sex act?

JA: Yes.

MG: How long a time would you estimate?

JA: A few hours, I'm not certain how long.

MG: Did you bring the condoms yourself or where did you get it?

JA: I think it was Anna's.

MG: Do you remember where she kept the condoms?

JA: No.

MG: How did you get the condom?

JA: I'm uncertain who put the condom on so I can't say.

MG: But you can't remember that you got the condom or something?

JA: No I can't remember but as I said, up until recently it was just an ordinary night. I had no reason to suspect I'd need to remember all the details from that night.

MG: How was your sexual coexistence after that night?

JA: **It was still pretty warm. There was one occasion after that night that Anna got two orgasms. We slept in the same bed.**

MG: And if I'd understood correctly so you didn't have sexual, you didn't have intercourse then?

JA: That is correct.

MG: And nothing happened during the time you lived with her after that first night?

JA: No there was no intercourse, that's correct. But other sexual activities, yes.

MG: **Were you ever rejected by Anna?**

JA: **In which way?**

MG: **That she rejected a sexual invite from you?**

JA: **Yes sometimes but in no significant way. No nothing that would be abnormal.**

MG: If we can go back to the first night. Did you ejaculate?

JA: Yes.

MG: So now I'll ask Ewa if you have anything you want to discuss.

EO: No.

MG: Leif, something you want to ... ?

LS: I have a couple of questions.

MG: Yes.

LS: At what time of the day did you have sex, what time was it approximately?

JA: Late at night and early in the morning.

LS: What would you say, approximately what time? Three, four, five … ?

JA: Between 23:00 and 05:00.

LS: OK. Was there any alcohol?

JA: No.

LS: Neither you nor her?

JA: Yes, I don't remember that I'd drunk any larger quantity. We can have had wine with dinner. But it wasn't en evening where we drank a lot.

LS: Were either of you inebriated?

JA: Not enough so I'd notice. I'd have noticed if either of us had been inebriated.

LS: When did you first hear from Anna about the issue we're discussing today?

JA: I've never heard precisely this issue directly from Anna. Today is the first time I get an exact description of it.

LS: So all the time you lived with Anna, from Friday to Friday and you had various sexual relations, so she said nothing about a broken condom?

JA: No nothing at all.

LS: Yes, I have no further questions.

MG: Then there's one more question popping up for me. Who was it who, shall we say, took the initiative to your getting closer to each other?

JA: Anna.

MG: How did that take place?

JA: She said I was to sleep in her bed.

MG: And things started in her bed?

JA: Yes that's correct.

MG: Were there any approaches from either of you before you got to bed?

JA: No.

MG: Did Anna say anything?

JA: No she didn't say anything but that was nothing unusual.

MG: And what do you mean by 'unusual'?

JA: They were just things you expected of a lover.

MG: And what were your plans when you were ready for bed then?

JA: After Anna had ...

MG: No before that.

JA: Before.

MG: Yes you say you got an invitation to her bed.

JA: Yes that's correct.

MG: Where had you planned to sleep before she invited you to the bed?

JA: Either on the floor or ... I don't know, it's Anna's flat.

MG: How long had you lived with Anna before this evening or lived alone in the flat?

JA: Yes, I'd lived in the flat because Anna was away. One day when she was away. I got the keys three, four days beforehand. I had access to the flat but I didn't sleep there. Anna, she sad that ... No I don't want to talk about this, for I don't believe this has anything to do with the case so I don't want to talk about private matters if they have no bearing on the case.

MG: Nobody has a follow-up question for this? OK then, is there anything you want to say before we conclude the interrogation?

JA: Yes.

MG: Go ahead.

JA: I was contacted by a mutual friend of Anna's and mine on Friday the 20th. It was a woman named Sonja who was at the hospital. She said something about DNA and the police. And I was very upset to hear this. No one was making any claims, it'd be a long narrative if I were to get into this. It doesn't seem relevant.

MG: OK so we hereby conclude the interrogation.

JA: We can always continue if it's needed? But the main thing is that I and others got to hear a lot of unbelievable lies. And got to hear I was to meet Sonja on Saturday afternoon to discuss the matter. Anna had no accusations and no one had any intention of going to the police and so forth. That's how I expected things to remain until I heard the news in *Expressen*.

MG: Right ... OK then. The interrogation is concluded. The time is 18:37.

---

[1] See http://lawline.se/answers/3119.

CHAPTER 4:
THE INTERROGATION OF PETRA ORNSTEIN

TUESDAY 7 SEPTEMBER 2010

THE INVESTIGATION OF PETRA ORNSTEIN

The interrogation of Petra Ornstein was conducted by Ewa Olofsson by telephone on 7 September and 8 September (18 days after the case was filed) and all told took 45 minutes.

Ewa Olofsson also acted as chief interrogator and police interrogation witness in some of the recorded interrogations including that of Julian Assange.

In contrast to the audio recording of Julian Assange's interrogation, but as for Sofia Wilén and Anna Ardin, this interrogation is a 'conceptual interrogation' ('konceptförhör') and takes the form of a narrative.

Signed by:	
Police authority:	Stockholm municipality
Date signed:	
Unit:	1/NJ On duty section
Journal #:	0201-K246336-10
Interrogated:	Ornstein, Petra
The interrogated is:	Witness
Civil registration #:	
Identify confirmed:	No
Relation to the suspect - complainant - witness:	
Interpreter:	
Language:	
Suspected crime / reason for interrogation:	Information about case K246336-10
Advised of suspicion:	
Advised of right to attorney:	
Defender/representative is desired:	
Defender/representative is present:	
Accepts defender provided by the court:	
Chief interrogator:	Ewa Olofsson
Date:	2010-09-07
Interrogation commenced:	15:25
Interrogation concluded:	15:50
Place of interrogation:	Telephone
Type of interrogation:	RB 23:6[1]
Method of interrogation:	
Interrogation witness:	
Transcribed by:	EO

Petra said she and Anna are good friends and that they took a train ride together on 11 August. Anna then told her Julian Assange would be living in her flat when he came to Sweden. Anna would be out of town.

Anna rang Petra the Saturday after and invited Petra to a crayfish party they were going to have for Julian at Anna's place. Anna also told her she'd had a wild weekend and had sex with Julian. Anna also mentioned Julian ejaculated in her but Petra was unsure of exactly what Anna was trying to say. Anna told her Julian broke a condom when they had sex but Petra interpreted it to mean Julian had broken it by mistake. Not until Sunday did Petra understand Anna was saying Julian broke the condom deliberately.

Petra was at the crayfish party and everything was normal and Petra met Julian for the first time. Petra hadn't sensed that Julian and Anna had something going at the party. Petra didn't speak very much with Julian.

Petra and Anna met on Sunday to work together. Petra asked Anna how things were, how things were going with Julian, if they'd had sex again, and if in such case it had been good. Anna told her they'd not had more sex because Anna didn't feel secure and then Anna told her what had happened. Anna told her story in a completely different way than previously, told her Julian had been unpleasant and amongst other things broken a necklace when they had sex. Anna had told Julian to take it easy but he just continued.

Anna also told Petra that she believed Julian had himself broken the condom they used. Petra said that she was ashamed because she hadn't understood and listened better to what Anna was actually saying during their Saturday telephone call when Anna told her about Julian. Petra had herself interpreted it, when Anna told the story, that Julian had thought it was hot whilst Anna thought it went beyond what she herself desired.

The most remarkable thing according to Petra was that Anna told her she hadn't been able to move when she and Julian had sex because Julian held onto her. Anna said she'd decided Julian should fuck her until he came because that was the simplest solution.

The story with the condom according to Petra sounded like another story which was also creepy but the most unpleasant thing according to Petra was the violence which made it unpleasant for Anna to have sex with Julian. Petra didn't get the impression that Anna had been afraid of Julian but it had instead been 'uncomfortable' and he hadn't treated her with respect. Julian didn't check to see what Anna wanted. Petra interpreted this to mean that Anna wasn't afraid but experienced the situation as a 'hassle'. He didn't anchor what he did with what she wanted and didn't care about her and lacked respect and used too much violence.

Anna said she could hardly move but could move enough to make sure Julian was wearing a condom. When Anna told the story she showed Petra with her head how she could see Julian's genitals. Anna said that they then had sex and then went beyond the limits when Anna lost interest. Julian then had sex with Anna until he came and then she felt how things ran out of her nether regions and she also saw how Julian's condom was rolled up at the root. Julian had then avoided Anna's questions.

After Sunday and during the following week Petra and Anna talked a lot about Julian. Petra learned a lot of things such as Julian doesn't take showers, he doesn't flush the toilet, and more. Anna also told her on Wednesday or Thursday that Julian had showered and also found another woman he slept over with. When they talked about Julian still living with Anna, Petra interpreted this to mean Anna wanted Julian to leave her flat in a few days but for some reason he was still there. Julian wanted to continually postpone his moving out despite her efforts.

Petra didn't think Anna was afraid of Julian. Anna didn't say anything about him being aggressive or dangerous but Anna wanted him out of her flat because of his behaviour and because the flat was rather small. Petra herself met Julian on two occasions, first at the crayfish party and then at a dinner the day after.

Anna rang Petra on Friday 20 August right after the other girl contacted Anna. Anna told her the other girl had told her she'd been raped by Julian. According to Anna, there were a number of similarities between their stories. What Petra primarily meant and what Anna told her was that Julian also had sex without a condom with the other girl. The other girl wanted sex (but with a condom) but Julian had seen to it they had sex without a condom against her wishes. Anna rang Petra and updated her because she herself hadn't planned on filing a complaint against Julian but she wanted to support the other girl.

Petra said the whole story got more and more uncomfortable for her and she's accused herself of not understanding from the beginning so she could have supported Anna right away.

Petra didn't know who the other girl was and still doesn't know. Anna said it was the same girl Julian had travelled to see after he had his shower.

Read back and approved. Chief interrogator's comments: the interrogation was paused 2010-09-07 15:50 and resumed 2010-09-08 13:10 and concluded 2010-09-08 13:50.

---

[1] See http://lawline.se/answers/3119.

CHAPTER 5:
THE INTERROGATION OF HANNA ROSQUIST
WEDNESDAY 8 SEPTEMBER 2010

THE INTERROGATION OF HANNA ROSQUIST

Hanna Rosquist was a friend of Sofia who had known her since childhood. The interrogation with Hanna was conducted on the telephone by Mats Gehlin on 8 September (19 days after the case was filed).

The protocol submitted by Gehlin states the interrogation began at 04:40 in the morning and concluded at 10:05 the same day. Considering the brevity of the interrogation, it's likely Gehlin is guilty of a typo and not correcting it and the correct start time is instead 09:40.

As for Sofia Wilén, Anna Ardin and Petra Ornstein, this interrogation is a 'conceptual interrogation' ('konceptförhör') in the form of a narrative.

Signed by:	
Police authority:	Stockholm municipality
Date signed:	
Unit:	1KU/F Domestic violence group
Journal #:	0201-K246336-10
Interrogated:	Rosquist, Hanna Mailies
The interrogated is:	Witness
Civil registration #:	
Identify confirmed:	No
Relation to the suspect - complainant - witness:	
Interpreter:	
Language:	
Suspected crime / reason for interrogation:	Interrogated as witness concerning what she's observed about the event
Advised of suspicion:	
Advised of right to attorney:	
Defender/representative is desired:	
Defender/representative is present:	
Accepts defender provided by the court:	
Chief interrogator:	Mats Gehlin
Date:	2010-09-08
Interrogation commenced:	04:40
Interrogation concluded:	10:05
Place of interrogation:	Telephone
Type of interrogation:	RB 23:6[1]
Method of interrogation:	
Interrogation witness:	
Transcribed by:	EO

Hanna states she's a childhood friend of Sofia. They've known each other since they were 11-12 years old. They lived and still live in Enköping. They meet or speak with each other regularly.

Hanna states that several weeks before the incident, Sofia talked about WikiLeaks and Julian Assange. Sofia admired his work and the WikiLeaks organisation. Sofia said he seemed good and smart as well as courageous when he's threatened because of his work.

On a later occasion Sofia told Hanna she'd seen Assange was to give a lecture in Sweden and she was going to attend. Hanna doesn't know how Sofia got a ticket to the lecture. She thinks Sofia just went there or reserved a seat in some way.

Hanna got an SMS message after the lecture from Sofia. Sofia was euphoric she'd been allowed to tag along to the lunch afterwards. She sat next to Assange and got to chat with him. Hanna knows that they also hung out after the lunch and can have gone to the museum but Hanna isn't certain. Hanna doesn't know what can have happened at the museum.

Hanna next spoke with Sofia on the morning Assange slept over at Sofia's. She can't remember if it was a phone call or SMS messages. Sofia said things didn't feel good and she wanted him gone. Sofia said Assange changed when he arrived at her place and had become an entirely different person and Sofia regretted letting him sleep over.

Sofia told Hanna she felt worse and worse after the incident. She told her the uncomfortable part was that Assange had unprotected sex with her when she was asleep. Sofia also said Assange had nagged and tried to have unprotected sex with Sofia during the night but Sofia got him to wear a condom. Sofia had spoken to Assange several times about condoms.

Sofia also told Hanna that Assange talked strangely, as if he wanted Sofia to get pregnant. He said things as if he wanted to make women pregnant. He supposedly said he preferred virgins because then he'd be the first one to make them pregnant.

Hanna asked Sofia why she didn't push Assange away when she understood he didn't have a condom. Sofia replied that she was so shocked and paralysed and couldn't really understand what was happening. She'd tried talking to him.

Hanna is certain Sofia wouldn't let things happen just because she admired him and he was a celebrity. But it can have meant something that he was older. Hanna doesn't know if Sofia was afraid of Assange.

Hanna says she'd seen in the newspaper that Sofia knew the other woman and she asked Sofia about this. Sofia told her 'yes now I do - but not before the lecture'.

Hanna says Sofia wanted Assange to take an STD test. Sofia took a test but it takes a lot longer to get the results. Things would go faster if Assange took a test.

Hanna doesn't know how it happened that Sofia went to the police.

Read back and approved.

---

[1] See http://lawline.se/answers/3119.

CHAPTER 6:
THE INTERROGATION OF KAJSA BORGNÄS

WEDNESDAY 8 SEPTEMBER 2010

THE INTERROGATION OF KAJSA BORGNÄS

The interrogation of Kajsa Borgnäs, a business associate of Anna Ardin who was at the crayfish party that night, was conducted on the telephone by Ewa Olofsson on 8 September (19 days after the case was filed). The interrogation began at 09:30 and concluded at 10:15.

Ewa Olofsson also acted as chief interrogator and police interrogation witness in some of the recorded interrogations.

As for Sofia Wilén, Anna Ardin, Petra Ornstein and Hanna Rosquist (but not Julian Assange), this interrogation is a narrative 'conceptual interrogation'.

Signed by:	
Police authority:	Stockholm municipality
Date signed:	
Unit:	1KU/F Domestic violence group
Journal #:	0201-K246336-10
Interrogated:	Borgnäs, Kajsa Hannele Elisabeth
The interrogated is:	Witness
Civil registration #:	
Identify confirmed:	No
Relation to the suspect - complainant - witness:	
Interpreter:	
Language:	
Suspected crime / reason for interrogation:	Information about complaint K 246336-10
Advised of suspicion:	
Advised of right to attorney:	
Defender/representative is desired:	
Defender/representative is present:	
Accepts defender provided by the court:	
Chief interrogator:	Ewa Olofsson
Date:	2010-09-08
Interrogation commenced:	09:30
Interrogation concluded:	10:15
Place of interrogation:	
Type of interrogation:	RB 23:6[1]
Method of interrogation:	Telephone
Interrogation witness:	
Transcribed by:	EO

Kajsa says she and Anna are good friends and Kajsa met Anna Tuesday 10 August. Anna told her they were going to try to get Julian Assange to Sweden and Kajsa said she'd also like to meet him even though she couldn't attend the lecture. They agreed to try to meet on Saturday and hopefully with Julian.

Kajsa later heard Julian was coming and on Saturday 14 August Kajsa and Anna spoke and decided they'd have a crayfish party and Julian would be there. Anna didn't tell her anything about her relationship with Julian.

Kajsa came to the party with her friend Alexandra at 19:00 on Saturday evening. Kajsa had amongst other things asked Anna if she was going to sleep with Julian, this because Anna is single and Anna and Kajsa have talked a lot about sex previously. Anna told her she already had done it but Anna said it was the worst screw she'd ever had. Anna also told Kajsa that Kajsa could move in and take Julian if she wanted.

Julian was terribly flirty at the party and even hit on Kajsa. Kajsa said that she nevertheless sensed an affinity between Anna and Julian at the same time Julian was flirting with Kajsa and probably other girls too. A girl even rang him on one or more occasions. Kajsa left the party at 03:00 in the morning. Julian wanted to accompany her but he didn't get to.

At some point, most likely during the party, Anna told her Julian had held her hands when they had sex, had held her hands up by her ears, and that had been uncomfortable. Anna not only thought that was the world's worst fuck but also that it had been violent. Anna showed her with her arms how she was lying when Julian held her. Kajsa had thought it was uncomfortable and not too cool but nothing more.

Kajsa and Anna spoke sometime during the following week and Kajsa asked Anna about Julian. Kajsa had wondered why Julian lived with her because Kajsa thought he was leaving the country. Anna didn't answer the question directly but admitted Julian was still there.

75

Kajsa and Anna were at a party together on Friday 20 August but this was after the police complaints and everything had already happened. Anna said she received an SMS message from the other girl who wanted to get in touch with Julian. Anna had understood what had happened and then they talked with each other. Anna said she and the other girl decided to go to the police because the other girl wanted to file a complaint of rape and Anna would follow along for support.

Then it was found out the police had even filed a complaint regarding Anna and the police had interpreted things to mean Anna was also a rape victim. That was also when Anna told her she thought Julian at first didn't want a condom and that they'd fought over that and then Anna rolled over. Then Julian put on a condom that Anna believed he'd broken later on during sex because she heard a snapping sound. Anna heard the sound after he'd pulled out during the act. Anna checked and ascertained the condom was still there.

Anna had been sad and reflective for she wondered how she would explain in a courtroom that she let him go on living with her despite what had happened. Anna also said she found it uncomfortable having him live there and she'd amongst other things vomited on a few occasions because she thought it was so uncomfortable.

Kajsa said the feeling she got was that Anna thought the situation was uncomfortable but not creepy or threatening. That was the feeling Kajsa got before Friday 20 August when she got to know everything.

Read back and approved.

---

[1] See http://lawline.se/answers/3119.

CHAPTER 7:

THE INTERROGATION OF KATARINA SVENSSON

MONDAY 13 SEPTEMBER 2010

THE INTERROGATION OF KATARINA SVENSSON

The interrogation of Katarina Svensson was conducted by Mats Gehlin in person on 13 September, 24 days after the case was filed.

Mats Gehlin had also acted as chief interrogator or police interrogation witness in some of the recorded interrogations, including that of Julian Assange.

The 'conceptual interrogation' began at 09:09 and concluded at 09:25.

Signed by:	
Police authority:	Stockholm municipality
Date signed:	
Unit:	1KU/F Domestic violence group
Journal #:	0201-K246314-10
Interrogated:	Svensson, Katarina Sonja Christina
The interrogated is:	Witness
Civil registration #:	
Identify confirmed:	No
Relation to the suspect - complainant - witness:	
Interpreter:	
Language:	
Suspected crime / reason for interrogation:	Information about complaint K 246336-10
Advised of suspicion:	
Advised of right to attorney:	
Defender/representative is desired:	
Defender/representative is present:	
Accepts defender provided by the court:	
Chief interrogator:	Mats Gehlin
Date:	2010-09-13
Interrogation commenced:	09:09
Interrogation concluded:	09:25
Place of interrogation:	Bergsgatan 48, Domestic violence group
Type of interrogation:	RB 23:6[1]
Method of interrogation:	Conceptual
Interrogation witness:	
Transcribed by:	EO

Katarina says she knows Sofia through work. They're 'better colleagues'. Katarina says she and Sofia began work there at the natural history museum about two years ago and had hourly wages. Katarina now has a monthly salary but Sofia still works by the hour.

Katarina says she's had a lot explained to her about the case. She didn't know Sofia and Assange had been at the museum. She says Sofia tried to ring her but she hadn't had her phone with her at the time. Sofia told her what happened when next they worked together.

Sofia told her she'd been at a lecture with Assange and there'd been a lunch afterwards. Assange went back to Sofia's flat after the lunch. Sofia said Assange wanted to have sex with her but Sofia said she didn't want sex without a condom.

Sofia said that when she was lying half asleep, she woke up to discover Assange was inside her. Sofia then asked him what he was wearing and Assange was to have replied 'I am wearing you'. Katarina said Sofia didn't notice he entered her but it was when he was already inside she woke up. Katarina said that Sofia didn't resist because she thought it was too late. Sofia also said she doesn't have sex with Assange but rather Assange had sex with her.

Sofia told Katarina Assange didn't want to leave in the morning and Sofia was forced to take a sick day from work because she didn't want to leave Assange alone in the flat as she didn't know him.

Katarina says they spoke about many intimate things and already before this incident Sofia told her she doesn't have sex without a condom. This to protect herself against diseases and pregnancy.

Katarina says Sofia has felt bad after the incident and that this feeling has been exacerbated by the attention of the media.

Read back and approved.

---

[1]See http://lawline.se/answers/3119.

CHAPTER 8:
THE INTERROGATION OF JOHANNES WAHLSTRÖM

MONDAY 20 SEPTEMBER 2010

THE INTERROGATION OF JOHANNES WAHLSTRÖM

Ewa Olofsson (EO) conducted the interrogation on 20 September (31 days after the case was filed) starting at 09:42 and concluding at 11:10. Mats Gehlin (MG) acted as police interrogation witness.

Johannes Wahlström is the son of Israel Shamir. He freelances for Aftonbladet *and worked for Jesper Huor and Bosse Lindquist on the* SVT *documentary* WikiRebels. *Johannes spent the early spring of 2010 in London with Julian Assange and the WikiLeaks team.*

Johannes also helped conduct a major investigation into the affairs of the powerful Bonnier publishing family after the diplomatic crisis in 2009 broke.

The interrogation of the Swedish journalist Johannes Wahlström is by far the most comprehensive and extensive in the entire case file. Like Julian Assange's interrogation (but in contrast to all the interrogations up to this point), it's an audio-recorded interrogation; so all the utterances, pauses, and non-words are included. Yet it's by far the most revelatory part of the entire case. Consequently, it will take quite a lot of work to read (as it was to translate and transcribe).

But it should be worth it.

Signed by:	
Police authority:	Stockholm municipality
Date signed:	
Unit:	1KU/F Domestic violence group
Journal #:	0201- K246336-10
Interrogated:	Wahlström, Johann
The interrogated is:	Witness
Civil registration #:	
Identify confirmed:	No
Relation to the suspect - complainant - witness:	
Interpreter:	
Language:	
Suspected crime / reason for interrogation:	Witness interrogation for the cases K 246314-10 and K 246336-10.
Advised of suspicion:	
Advised of right to attorney:	
Defender/representative is desired:	
Defender/representative is present:	
Accepts defender provided by the court:	
Chief interrogator:	Ewa Olofsson
Date:	2010-09-20
Interrogation commenced:	09:42
Interrogation concluded:	11:10
Place of interrogation:	City police, Bergsgatan 48, Stockholm
Type of interrogation:	RB 23:6[1]
Method of interrogation:	Audio tape recording
Interrogation witness:	Gehlin, Mats
Transcribed by:	JW

EO: OK, do you have any questions before we begin?

JW: Yes, it's uh, well partly a clarification which, which maybe I want to make and partly a question which touches on this case.

EO: Hmmm ...

JW: And the clarification has to do with my professional role. That is to say I am a journalist. And in some cases which, which have to do with my practicing my profession and cases which have to do with my sources, I can't reveal my sources. Uh, I don't think that it will be particularly relevant in this interrogation but, uh, yes that's the clarification.

When we come to the actual interrogation so, um, a little bit also because of what I just mentioned right now uh, so I'm curious about in which way this interrogation will possibly be made accessible to the media. Please tell me now.

EO: That, that the judicial system reviews each and every document which someone requests.

JW: I might not understand the judicial games in this matter in such case but if I have not understood, or if I have believed that it has functioned uh, so it's then the interrogations are covered by the secrecy act until the day when uh, when a case is, or a what shall we say, a prosecution is begun or?

MG: Yes or, a prosecution ...

EO: Prosecution ...

JW: Goes to a prosecution.

EO: Precisely. And then we always respect the confidentiality of the preliminary investigation.

JW: Precisely.

EO: Yes.

JW: So is it so that this interrogation will be kept secret until a prosecution has begun?

MG: It works like this, all confidentiality shall, it's like this that this is a public document according to the first principle that they're public with respect to all documents within all agencies.

JW: Hmmm ...

MG: If it happens that someone requests a document, then it's so that then everything must be in principle reviewed again, in other words all text must be checked for secrecy, in other words the preliminary investigation. Now it's so that now it's very strict secrecy in this case, so that it, it can be so that a document can be released but maybe it's entirely blackened. For if someone requests a document then they're supposed to get a document.

JW: Hmmm. That, the reason I ask this is that I have understood, now I've been out of the country a lot, but I've understood that uh, there have been interrogations that have been released and above all else to, to a tabloid newspaper uh, and now I'm thinking about *Expressen*. Uh, and I don't know if these interrogations have been released in accordance with the secrecy act or if there are leaks in your building here. But for me it's very important that if I am going to talk about my journalistic profession, uh, and if the contacts I have in my profession that, uh, that you can guarantee in some way that during a certain time so this won't, yeah, let's say tomorrow be leaked to *Expressen*.

MG: Nothing has been leaked. All has been released.

JW: So nothing, there haven't been any leaks?

MG: There have been no leaks and everything that's come out, in other words from it coming to this group. All documents that have been released have been released on request. And you know yourself how that's done most likely ...

JW: Hmmm ...

MG: ... That you've requested documents. So that, that *Expressen* has and that *Aftonbladet* has received as well, this is on the request of, in other words after review according to the secrecy act and then it's been blackened out. If one says, that which is blackened out in the newspapers that's what the police have done, that's not the newspaper.

JW: Hmmm ...

MG: But it's the police who have done a confidentiality review huh and that has occurred through, in the first place, from the beginning part of the city police unit after that it's moved over to the central judicial unit on county level now who handle all these things huh.

JW: But you mean in other words that it, the interrogations which have up to now been published in the newspapers that they are public to the degree that, that the newspapers could publish during an ongoing preliminary, preliminary interrogation?

MG: Yes it was the judicial unit in the city police from the beginning. Then it went up to the central judicial unit. But that is in other words, each document that's been released has been released on the request of private citizens and the press.

JW: Yeah.

MG: Hmmm.

EO: I can also add that what's said in here today it's we three who have that information. In addition this interrogation will be transcribed by one of our colleagues who will also be privy to what is said, what's been said in here. So that ...

MG: And it's the same girl who's written everything.

EO: Who has, who has transcribed all interrogations.

JW: Hmmm ...

MG: So OK then.

EO: Anything else you ...

JW: No that, let's, let's get to work.

EO: Yes. Yes precisely. Precisely. And I'd ask you to begin to tell us of your contact with Julian Assange. And, uh, yes in connection with and before he came to Sweden.

JW: Uh, I've worked with Julian Assange uh, on assignment from Swedish Television. In a, uh, an ongoing documentary which I don't have the authority to, to talk about. Uh and I ...

EO: Yes.

JW: ... And I met him a, uh, shall we say if I remember exactly but it's probably approximately, let's say a week before he comes to Sweden I met him in England. And after that he came to Sweden and I returned a day or twelve hours later approximately. Or ...

EO: Hmmm.

JW: You said contacts before he came here.

EO: Precisely. What's it called, hang out, were you involved in his assignments here in Sweden ...

JW: As ...

EO: So to speak, were you, were you in England and met him because of his assignments here?

JW: I was in England and met him on assignment from Swedish Television.

EO: OK. Hmmm. Had you, did you organise things for his visit here in Sweden?

JW: No.

EO: Nothing?

JW: That depends on what you mean ...

EO: No I'm thinking about his living conditions on his, what assignments he had, possibly interviews.

JW: No but on the other hand I was aware of what there were, were for assignment and living conditions and things like that. And I helped make contacts, that I can say. Uh, partly with the Swedish Brotherhood movement which then came to invite him to, to Sweden. Uh, I had email contact with Anna Ardin then who was press secretary, or who most likely still is, in the Brotherhood movement.

Uh, and she, uh, for practical reasons sent the airplane tickets to, to me, for him. And beyond that, the purely practical matters were taken care of by, uh, her and the others of the Brotherhood movement, I have no clear idea of how, how that works administratively with them, uh ... What I had explained to me then that they would partly invite him to a seminar and partly take care of his living expenses up to a few days after the seminar.

EO: Hmmm. OK and so then you return to Sweden, uh, a half day you said ...

JW: Hmmm.

EO: ... After Julian. And do you make, have you contact directly when you return to Sweden or?

JW: Yes that, I arrived in the night so I think we made contact in the morning. That's to say one more, one more night later.

EO: And when was that, do you remember?

JW: I could look in my almanac. Uh ... But, counting backwards what it was, uh ... In other words you've surely got your documents on when he came to Sweden so that it, uh..

EO: This, the seminar was on Saturday.

JW: On Saturday.

EO: Yes.

JW: And ... Either it was a Thursday or so it was a Friday. Most likely so, most likely I returned on Thursday evening. Or Thursday night. And so, and so we met on Friday.

EO: Hmmm.

JW: Uh, that's my recollection, if you don't want me to look in my almanac.

EO: Yes you can of course look in your almanac please so we can clarify it all.

JW: No guarantees I've written down the date.

EO: No.

JW: Dum, dum, dum, dum ... What date was the seminar?

EO: The 14th.

JW: The 14th. Um ... OK let's see, uh ... Precisely, that is to say in other words that I, uh, flew home on the 11th at night. And then in other words I met him on Thursday.

EO: On Thursday yes.

JW: That's my recollection.

EO: Hmmm. And then from Thursday where you had contact and met during the following week, during that week and the following week?

JW: Yeah we met during, uh, as I remember it every day until I left the week after.

EO: What day did you leave?

JW: (Clears throat.)

EO: I'm difficult.

JW: I don't remember if it was the 18th or the 19th. Uh, can check in my, my plane tickets if you want. Or wait a minute, I can check in my almanac. Uh ... I think I left on the 18th at night.
EO: Hmmm.

JW: Left Sweden and then I've been away until the 15th, that's to say until a few days ago.

EO: Yes precisely. And then from your arrival in Sweden the 12th, or the 11th, 12th when you make contact.

JW: Hmmm.

EO: How did you associate, how did you meet, in what context?

JW: We collaborated at a number of meetings. Uh, of a journalistic nature so to speak.

EO: Were you also at the meeting on Saturday the 14th?

JW: Saturday the 14th ...

EO: With the Brotherhood movement.

JW: Yes, I was, I was.

EO: OK. What, what was your impression of Julian as a person?

JW: Uh ... Impression of Julian as a person. Uh, that's a big, um, intelligent individual. He is, uh, friendly and warm you can say. Um ... He, um ... Sorry, now my phone is ringing. Uh ... Yeah so you could ask some leading questions if you want instead, it's easier for me to reply to them.

EO: No I'm thinking you met him quite a lot, rather frequently during ...

JW: Hmmm.

EO: A period when, did you have time, did you have time so to speak to get to know each other any better ...
JW: On a personal level?

EO: Yes precisely. More than work or?

JW: Yes I think I have a feel for, for how he is as a person, yes.

EO: Hmmm.

JW: I think I can say that.

EO: Hmmm, hmmm.

JW: And ... Um ... He is, uh ... Is a person who in certain aspects is very capable and very skillful. And in certain regards uh, so he can for example have difficulty finding the way if he's walking in, in town, uh for he gets so deeply into conversations. And, uh ... He has a uh, a way to bring out a kind of um, goodwill or what you want to express it as. Because, uh ... Yeah I don't know, there, there are certain people who have a sort of charisma that makes people want to be nice to them. So something like that. And he himself is very, in other words simply put, nice.

EO: Hmmm.

JW: I can uh ... You asked me as stated if I was there, there at the meeting with the Brotherhood movement.

EO: Yes precisely, hmmm.

JW: We can talk about that. But I'd also like to say something in connection with, with this particular case. And, uh, and the questions as stated around it.

EO: Hmmm.

JW: So uh, so I noticed when I was in London ... I noticed something that for me was very startling because we in journalism are uh, not used to, as regards celebrities in a way that, that one can be like in the music industry or whatever. Uh, but what I discovered very quickly was that, um, uh, that Julian he awakened some sort of, uh, some sort of celebrity interest amongst, amongst girls.

And uh, above all amongst girls who, who I'd expect to be uh ... As more, one can say, professional in character. Now I'm talking about how things were in London. Uh, and, yes they, they hit on him, that's how I can put it. Uh ... Looked a little as if like this, yes there were journalists from very, very prestigious publications in other words that, that uh, that behaved like school girls when they, when they looked at him. Giggling, trying to hug. Try, what's the word, put their hands on his thighs. Yeah, yeah for my ...

EO: What ...

JW: For my part it looked very very strange.

EO: What did he make of it?

JW: He, uh ... He was mostly unmoved. He smiled and thought that, the situation looked, seemed to be amusing, I think he found it nice. Uh, but I remember specifically a situation where we sat at a, a meeting. Or it was an, an informal meeting I can say, but nonetheless which was in, of a work context. Uh and as people can sometimes do with uh, with a glass of wine in their hand. And so there were maybe 15 people who were sitting at that, uh, that meeting. And we discussed all the issues that had to do with our professional roles. And uh, and in, in relation to it, certain materials we were working on.

And two women who were uh, who also worked in, in uh, journalism with this material. They sat down very quickly right next to him. And um, and it was obvious that, that they were, from either side, trying to tug, to see who would gain his, his interest. Uh, but he seemed more interested in discussing ethics in journalism, politics, and, so those, those issues. But it looked really strange, I can say that. From my point of view.

EO: Hmmm.

JW: Particularly as I knew who those two women were. Um, and particularly as their assignment at that place was of a journalistic nature.

EO: Did you and Julian talk about this later?

JW: Uh, we talked with him about, about this later. And I noted that uh, that he didn't, not really, not really rebuffed either the invites that, that those women came with. And without knowing anything about, about the details where they, what had happened or not happened so I told him in with all good intentions that I thought he should be extremely careful. For in his pressed situation uh, he can't know if it's a person he can trust or not. And um, in the political game which, which, which he is so used to or how you want to put it, what he's got involved in so it's far from unusual or for that matter unthinkable that someone can plan to, to create trouble for him through uh, sexual contacts.

And, so I talked with him a couple of times and I had a, a long serious conversation with him about this when we came to Sweden. Uh, which day it, most likely on Friday I'd guess.

EO: And why, why the long serious conversation?

JW: No it was just that uh, that it was ... I noticed that uh, that there was, that there was as for many, in other words if I'm going to describe it without in any way seeming contemptuous towards anyone, there were too many groupies of womanly character like circulating around him. Uh and even if he only talked with them the way he let them in like in his conversation uh, meant that he lowered his guard in a different way compared to if he'd be talking to you or you to me. Um, so that was very simply a, such a, such a discussion.

There are a number of examples in, in history where, where very well known, above all controversial figures have got into trouble with things like this. I think not in the least about Mordechai Vanunu, don't know if you know him.[2] He's the man who exposed Israel's nuclear weapons secret almost 20 years ago. He uh, he happened to, after he exposed the nuclear weapons secret he happened to meet a, a young girl whom he thought was really nice and cute and all of that. And she flirted with him very intensively and so she asked him if he'd like to follow along on a trip to Italy. And he did and then he was drugged and smuggled in a box to Israel and then spent 20 years in prison. It turned out she was a Mossad agent.

Uh and what Julian Assange and his organisation have been dealing with that's in no way less serious within world politics than what Mordechai Vanunu did. And for me so, so, he knew of this case. It wasn't unknown for him. But I felt it was important to point out that risk for him.

EO: Hmmm. Had he then, when you had that conversation, had, already had a relationship here in Sweden or in London that you knew about?

JW: I didn't know of his relationships in detail. I could only see uh, the way girls, uh, girls, uh, flocked to him.

EO: Hmmm. I understand. What, have you had, you say you had contact with Anna Ardin, mail-wise. Did you know each other ...

JW: No.

EO: ... Beforehand?

JW: No, we didn't know each other beforehand.

EO: How did you make contact?

JW: I suspect, without knowing for that matter, that uh, was most likely asked by her superiors to, to send the tickets to me. And how that contact happened uh, I don't know that, don't know ...

EO: No.

JW: And, and it's nothing I want to get into either because it has nothing to do with this interrogation.

EO: Have you, have you had any contact since you returned to Sweden?

JW: We had contact uh, the first time I met her was on Saturday morning. That's to say a few hours uh, before the seminar at the LO-borgen.

EO: Precisely, hmmm.

JW: And Anna Ardin, if she wrote to me or if I had it told to me afterwards, I can't remember, I was supposed to look in my computer I presume, uh, offer her flat to Julian Assange whilst he was here.. And uh ... I, I helped him as I said with, with a few practical things there. It had to do with, uh as I said partly turning over tickets and partly so I wanted simply put to find out where he was going when he was here.

Considering the Brotherhood movement invited him uh, so they agreed to see that, that he'd have a place to live. And then I heard there was an empty flat that belonged to the Brotherhood movement's press secretary, she'd be away. She'd be away until ... Until Saturday if I remember correctly. Uh, and in that way so, uh, so there'd be a place for him to, to stay. And, uh, at a later time either they or someone else would find in some way a place for him to move to.

Uh, it's easier if you help me with the date because I don't really have it in my head ...

EO: Hmmm. No ...

JW: And I haven't thought a lot about this, uh, during, during the past month considering I've been away. But what I remember very clearly was that uh, that Anna Ardin re, she was to return to Stockholm a day earlier. What day it was I don't remember, if it was Thursday or Friday. Uh, I'd guess it was Friday without uh, being able to put my hat on it. Uh ... And ... Yeah it was definitely Friday. And she, uh, she wanted to meet Julian considering he was living in her flat. But there was nothing wrong with his living there because she had somewhere else she could go. And that day we had a meeting with um ... A meeting with the representative of the Brotherhood movement. And he told me this, this thing.

EO: Yes it was he who informed ...

JW: He, he informed me ...

EO: OK, yeah yeah. Hmmm.

JW: ... Information that Anna would be returning a day earlier. But it was cool, Julian could go on living where he was, uh and she was going to live somewhere else. Uh, later at, during, a little later so uh, I heard that through Julian that, uh, that Anna Ardin had contacted him and wanted to meet, uh ... Before, before the seminar. And as I understood it so, my impression is that I, I directed him to her flat, uh, and then I went home. And it was probably in the evening but it wasn't night. Uh, and ...

EO: On Friday?

JW: On Friday.

EO: OK, hmmm.

JW: That's my recollection.

EO: Hmmm.

JW: And, and then she was supposed to uh, she and he were supposed to, supposed to meet up. Uh, then in the morning, on Saturday morning I was supposed to see that uh, to fetch Julian from the flat to show him the way to LO-borgen. The seminar was at 11:00 if I remember correctly. And that means I was most likely there about 09:00, 09:30, don't know exactly when it was.

And so uh, I ring the door. I know to start with that Julian would never find it. And secondly I knew he has a bit of a difficulty with punctuality. So I thought it was a friendly gesture to, to, and wake him. I was one of the only people in Sweden who knew where he was. So I rang the door and to my surprise Anna Ardin opened the door. And she ... She looked a bit, uh, a bit, what can I say, hmmm ... She looked, looked as if, that she hadn't expected to see me, that I can say. Uh, and I definitely didn't expect to see her, uh, in the morning. And I asked in a somewhat discreet way, uh, yeah what's it called had they, if they, if she had arrived now or not like ...

EO: But you understood it was Anna?

JW: I understood that ... She like introduced herself as Anna.

100

EO: Yes, OK hmmm.

JW: Uh, and so I went in the flat and saw, uh, saw a bed. Uh, it's a very small flat, um ... I have 35 square metres, one room and kitchen. Hers looked to be, to be, yeah but almost ten square metres less. So there was a relatively small sofa and a little bed. And uh, Julian sat in the room and she was dressed in the hall and met me. I made only a, a mental note of the fact that uh, yeah they've spent the night, spent the night in one way or another in uh, the flat. Uh, it's not a really big flat so there's not really any space for, for living in separate rooms.

Uh but I didn't get into that questioning, I was interested in seeing they arrived in time at the seminar. So Anna left a bit earlier. And then maybe a quarter of an hour later we left for, for the LO-borgen, me and Julian then in other words. Uh, shall we see, thinking back if there was anything more ...

EO: Did he say anything about the night?

JW: Absolutely not. Uh, firstly it's not my business to ask questions of a personal nature. Particularly not with a person I have a professional relationship with. And secondly so it's not, I felt that he wasn't a person who, who talked about private matters in that way. Uh, but there was a, a thin, thin, thin mattress. Which was about this thin without sheets or anything else that lay on the floor. Uh, I noted it for myself that, yeah maybe he slept on it. But I presumed, presumed it. Uh and that, I thought it was very strange that she had spent the night there. But nothing other than that.

Then we went to, uh, the seminar. And there were a lot of people, a huge press corps. Most of them, without knowing anything about the statistics but it looked like most of them in, in the seminar room were members of the journalist profession. Really a lot of cameras and video cameras and pens, dictaphones, and so forth. And Anna she helped with coordinating things, the practical details. And it went off as, as it should, nothing unusual.

And, and then when the seminar was over because there was a time frame where they were forced to leave the LO-borgen. And we went out and stood, in other words all of us including a lot of journalists stood outside, um, outside the building. And so Anna had made some sort of list, uh of journalists, who were permitted to do an interview there. And they were ticked off the list and it took like a long time. Uh, and ... Uh ... And so, during this time more and more people dropped off, went away. Uh but, uh, the idea was that, uh, I think his name was Peter Weiderud I think, he who's, who was responsible there at the Brotherhood movement. Uh, he and Anna Ardin and I and a journalist whose name is Donald Boström, we were the ones who uh, had had you can say all the original contacts with, partly with Julian and partly from the Brotherhood too. We were going to lunch after the seminar. And there were some people standing around after the journalists started leaving and there were only maybe one or two remaining. Uh and so I went up to, to, yeah his name is Peter Weiderud or?

MG: Uh if it's him with the Brotherhood movement.

JW: The Brotherhood movement yeah.

MG: Yeah we've had [inaudible] but it ...

JW: I'm maybe mixing up the names. Who was in charge?

EO: I'm not sure.

MG: I'm not sure either but it's nothing we ...

JW: No.

EO: I recognise it from before.

JW: At any rate, uh I go up to him and so I ask him, um, what, what's the plan. And so he says, yes we're going to go eat lunch and so he asks if I have any suggestions where to go. Then it's suggested we go to, uh, or I suggest we can go to Bistro Bohème which is like right next door. Uh and there are a few people who, who are still there and I ask like this, who are they. Yeah, no clue. Uh, and, and so I note in front a, a young girl[3] standing there in some sort of pink jacket. Uh, yeah she stands out in an, an unbelievable way you could say in this context. Totally shocking pink.

Uh, and, and so I ask who, something about yeah who, who is that. Uh, because she was standing too close, too close to the gang who'd organised the event. And so he says, no but she had, she's been helping here as, as a volunteer or an apprentice, something like that he said. Uh, OK I say, but you can see to it that she, that they leave. Because I mean I don't want any outsiders at our lunch. Uh, now it's been like everything from uh, politicians to journalists to like groupies who've been standing there for almost four hours. We can like go ourselves. So, yeah but she has, she has helped so much for free so that the least we can do is invite her to, to, to uh, to come along to the lunch.

Uh, to go back to what I mentioned before with my warning to Julian. For my part there were a lot of warning sirens going off just by what I saw of her. Uh, and that she suddenly ended up so close, uh, like that conversation climate that we're four people like sitting there and discussing sensitive issues. Uh so it's some person I don't know and I don't know who she is. Uh and suddenly she's following along on a, on a lunch.

Uh and, but about that, his name was Peter, he was in charge for the entire seminar he uh, he said that, no but she's joining us for lunch. And so I asked Anna the same thing if she knew who she was. And she said something like, uh, that she'd contacted the Brotherhood movement and asked if she could help out with anything. But that she herself didn't really know who it was. Uh, then ... Uh ... But that she, that she worked at, uh, the natural history museum or something like that.

Uh, yeah so we went to the lunch restaurant and if I remember correctly so it was so that the people I mentioned earlier, that's to say

103

it was Anna Ardin, it was me, Donald Boström, it was Julian Assange, and that young girl.[4]

EO: Do you remember her name?

JW: Yeah her name was Sofia. Uh, and ... She, she was put at the end of the table. Because I think practically speaking everyone felt she shouldn't really be there. Uh and so we discussed things together how we thought the seminar had gone uh, and some other matters like of a political and journalistic character.

Uh I noticed a really strange scene. Because she sat quiet through, through the entire lunch. She sat next to Julian. I think it was Peter, Julian, her, me, Anna, Donald. Uh, and she sat quiet during the entire lunch and nothing to chime in under, with the uh, in the topics we discussed. And sure enough, she broke into the conversation. And so she asked, she stared intently at Julian and so she asked, did you like, did you like your cheese sandwich or something like that. And I reacted, I don't remember if it was a cheese sandwich but it was something like that, something, something extraordinarily trivial. Uh and, and he reacted too. And he noticed she was sitting next to him. And so he looked at her, uh ... And so he said, uh, yeah do you want to taste it? And so she took a bite of his cheese sandwich. Uh, and (laughs) ... Yeah if you think if you're like sitting with a bunch of policemen like and then so there's someone there you don't really know who it is who takes a bite of your friend's cheese sandwich uh, you're a bit perplexed.

Uh then it ended, uh the meeting, after lunch the meeting ended. And, uh, me and Julian were going to go, to, in each our own directions. I think everyone went off in their own directions. But wait before that ended so we discussed um, something about Swedish traditions. And I said something about, yeah isn't it time for crayfish or something like that. Uh I suggested, one perhaps, it might be cool for Julian to see a Swedish crayfish party. I was onto Anna Ardin who sat next to me she said that, yes but I can fix a crayfish party. So within three minutes she'd made some calls and then after she hung up she said, yeah at so and so o'clock at my place it'll be a crayfish party and you're all invited. And it was really fast and very heartfelt and I thought it was really like nice. Above all like in some way when it was so unexpected.

Uh, so in any case we went off and I was supposed to fix some of my stuff but I walked along with Julian and the others went in their own directions. Anna went off to fix, uh, to fix the purchases of crayfish and spirits - was a bit difficult on Saturday right after lunch. Uh and ... Um ... And so I noted this young, young girl[5] Sofia following along. Partly, yes me and Julian.

EO: Hmmm.

JW: And, and I pull Julian a little bit to the side and so I ask him like this, what, who is that. And so he looks at me like this, yeah but she works for the Brotherhood movement. She said that, that she can help me get a cable for my computer like this. OK, yeah OK. So we walk together the three of us to a computer store and ask if they have one, yeah some type of cable that they want. Uh and they don't have one in the store, so we walk to another computer store and it's the same thing there, or else it's closed. Uh, and so I'm thinking, yeah but now she's done her thing and now she can leave.

Uh, but instead so, so she keeps Julian there and asks if he'd like to go and see where she works which is, I don't remember if it was the natural history museum but it was some sort of museum, some big museum in Stockholm. Uh, and he asks me, how do you say it, do you want me to go along with you and help you with some stuff or, uh, because I'd be glad to. I say, no but you go to the museum and we'll meet in the evening at the crayfish party.

Uh, so they head off to the museum. At any rate what I know. And, and I go off to do my stuff. Uh, then, uh towards, towards the evening I arrive at, uh, at Anna Ardin's. They've rung a few times and asked where I am, uh ... I was late, way late I guess. And so I arrive at that crayfish party to put it simply. So they've booked, or set out a table in the inner courtyard. Uh, in addition to Anna and Julian and Donald who are sitting there, there are two people from the

Pirate Party. Um, and another three, four girls and one guy, friends of Anna's. And I presumed that they in some way were, were either connected to the Brotherhood or in some other way, uh ... Yeah, or that it was simply put friends, I didn't think a lot about, about that issue.

Uh, and so the evening wears on. Uh, and so I note a, a curious uh, exchange, one can say. It's a very hearty evening, I can say that like already at once.

EO: Hmmm, hmmm.

JW: There's absolutely nothing, uh, hateful like or something like that, save for one thing. And it was then a friend of Anna Ardin's who sat quite a ways from me, uh, who made it very clear that partly she's a lesbian and partly had a, a very strong grudge towards men in general. Uh, and she says something like, she screams over the table to Anna that, uh, next time we'll have a crayfish party without men or something like that. So I just put that, that phrase in my memory. Then I asked a little half-joking like this, I spinned the issue further with, with Anna. Like this why would they want to do that. She said something like, yeah yeah but it's good when women can, can get together like only for themselves, be strong together or something like that.

Uh, and later on in the evening so, uh, I think I asked, uh, I asked Anna, um ... No I first asked Julian, uh, where, where he would, would spend the night.

EO: Hmmm.

JW: Uh and, and then he says, yeah I have a few offers. OK, OK, but everything seemed like fixed. And, and so he says, well I've been invited by one of those young ladies who, who, we, who we met before, Sofia. But there was a technical detail or something like that to be arranged before they could meet. I don't know what that technical detail was, I wasn't very interested in that, I just wanted to know if he had somewhere to sleep. Because if, if I was going to let him use my flat or something like that. Uh, and then I asked Anna if it was OK if he stayed at her place instead or if she wanted me to take him to my place. Uh she said, no no problem, he can, sure he can stay with me.

Uh and then the hour was very late, perhaps three or something like that and so everyone left except Julian and, and Anna. I helped carry up the last, last glasses and stuff. And, and then I said farewell to them in the flat. And then it was apparent that, that they both would be sleeping in the flat.

EO: Was there something, something between them that you noticed that evening?

JW: A, a strong friendship.

EO: OK.

JW: A very heartfelt friendship. There were no, no open flirtations that I saw. And that was why I didn't either, uh, or I got like the feeling somewhere from, uh, from Anna uh ... She, she wanted to take care of Julian in some way.

EO: Hmmm.

JW: I got an SMS message from her a few, a few days later. I don't remember exactly the day but it was something about, I can show it to you if you want. Uh, which was something like the, the, um ... Here. Uh, the 16th of August, that means ...

EO: Monday.

JW: Monday.

EO: Yes.

JW: Yes. We met the day before as well I'd think, Sunday. But at any rate there, an SMS message. Uh, and so on, this is a Monday morning and Julian and I were to meet with, uh, Swedish Television. And he [*sic*] messages me uh, that, uh, hi now I've told him three times he has to take a shower, he smells terrible I can't take it, you're his best Swedish friend, yeah that's her definition, can you figure out some way to solve this problem, thanks Anna. And so I answered something like hahaha, uh, yeah and so she replied again, haha OK, but you can get some hot Pirate girl to ... On the pretext to take him to her place or point it out yourself or something. I've, now I've at least forcibly washed his clothes.

Uh, and in the following days so, so uh, so we met every day. That's to say both Julian and Anna Ardin. Partly for work I'm involved in and partly to help with some interviews. And at this point Anna and Julian have developed a relationship where she is his, his like plastic mum. Or something like that. She sees to it that she can take care of his wash and sees he eats properly. Yeah she, she talks about it several times.

And, and um ... The same evening that I, or the evening before I leave, that's to say Tuesday I think, so I'd left Julian at a, a restaurant. And so Anna rings and so I say, yes he's there and there uh you can ... No she rings me like this. Asks me where he is, she was leaving work. And so I ask, uh, then she asks where he is and so I tell her, he's here. Uh and so I joke something about, yeah what was it, uh, we've become uh, we've become a sort of um ... Or yeah I say, you'll have to assume responsibility for our adopted child now. So she says, yeah, um, yeah I have for some time, often thought of adopting a child, I didn't know he'd be so, that he would be so grown up. But it's, it's like a very heartfelt like, a very heartfelt conversation.

EO: Hmmm.

JW: And then she leaves work and meets him.

EO: Does she express any desire to have him move out?

JW: I actually asked her every day. Uh, and I know it's not my business to ask a question like that. Uh but, but I try, I pull her away, pull her away a bit, a few, a few times. And so I ask her like this, is everything cool. In other words without going into detail here, do you, is it cool he's living there, do you want like for me to fix something else. Uh and so she says, no but it's, it's that he, he he doesn't like sleep at nights so that's a bit difficult, uh, and so he has a bit of difficulty taking care of his hygiene. Uh, but, no it's OK if he lives with me, it's, it's no problem, just so I know approximately how long it's going to be. Uh, but I think that question was asked by me, either three or four times. That's to say, uh, from the first time which, which was Saturday uh, until ...

EO: The day of the seminar, yeah precisely.

JW: The day of the seminar, Monday, Tuesday.

EO: Yes. Do Anna or Julian speak with you about them having a, having, or having had or that they're going to have a sexual relationship?

JW: Absolutely not.

EO: Neither of them?

JW: Absolutely not.

EO: No.

JW: And to be honest uh, so, uh, now that I know that it's come out, what's it called read in the evening tabloids just as you have ...

EO: Hmmm.

JW: That they evidently did have. Uh but it came as an absolute shock for me. Which possibly, now when I say, say this maybe shouldn't have happened. But for some reason so um, so she and I had such a relationship, partly with each other but partly in respect to Julian and it felt more like uh, yeah we helped out like with taking care of our guest. And just as improbable that I'd have a sexual relationship with Julian I felt that it would be that she would have one. Uh ... But ... Yes. I didn't think about that at all. Save the first, first uh, the first time when I discovered they were sleeping in the same flat. But after that so, so uh, I didn't think about it anymore.

EO: Did Julian meet another woman at this time? You've said he and Sofia went to, to her place of work on one occasion and that ...

JW: I don't know where they went, uh ...

EO: No but they talked about it.

JW: Hmmm.

EO: And then he was invited to sleep over at her place.

JW: Yes.

EO: But, did he do it?

JW: Um, I have no, no knowledge of what he actually, actually did. I knew we were going to meet ... Uh, yeah I can actually check this too, I got an SMS message from Anna in that regard too. Uh, I ask, uh ... Here. This is from the 17th of August, good morning, can you remind J that we have a meeting at noon at the journalists association, suspect he's asleep and unfortunately I can't pick him up today. That's me writing that. Anna Ardin answers, he's not here, he's planned to have sex with the cashmere girl every evening but not made it, maybe he finally found time yesterday? It's 09:40 the 17th of August. My reply ...

EO: The 17th of August?

JW: My reply the 17th of August, my reply, poor taste, do you have her number. Her reply, uncertain if he has any taste to be honest but she was cute. Not mentally fast enough according to J. But cashmere and breasts and idol worship compensate. No unfortunately not,

110

sofia.wilen@hotmail.com, works at the natural history museum that's all I know.

Uh, and so he missed that meeting we'd agreed to. Uh and I have to, I ask, I ask people to ring him during the day because I have a lot to do, otherwise. And then he turns up at about 14:00 I think. And so, so we move the meeting we were supposed to have at the journalists association to 16:00 in the evening instead.

Uh, and then, right when I spoke with him at lunchtime, in other words when this meeting was to have taken place at the journalists association, then I reach him by telephone. And so he tells me that, uh, he's stuck on a train. Uh, and that, uh, it would take a long time to get back, get back to town. So I suspected it was a commuter train or whatever it could be or something. And, yeah he'd calculated the time wrong to put it simply. This was don't forget with the chairman of the journalists association. So that it, in a Swedish context, so even if he's very well known in a Swedish context so it's difficult to organise these types of meetings and move them two hours this way or that.

EO: Hmmm. But no more talk about where he spent the night or with whom?

JW: I don't think I asked that question. Uh, and this has more to do with, with my attempt like to, uh ... Even if, if he has a friendship, what should I say, relationship in that regard like that one can go and, and, together to a crayfish party or like help him find things, whatever that can be, with all those things, so I didn't feel I wanted to know anything about his private life. But I made it clear that I thought it was uh, bad form to not come in time like to a meeting.

EO: When he'd moved out of Anna's flat, why did he do that and when, do you know?

JW: I left the country, I told you the date there ...

EO: Yes precisely, on Wednesday there ...

JW: So that then he was, as far as I knew still with Anna.

EO: OK.

JW: Uh ...

EO: After that ...

JW: He was going to leave, he was going to leave the country. And he was to leave the country the day after me. Or maybe it was the same day. Uh, so I understood, understood the plan. And, and then I asked even Anna as stated if it was, it was OK that he stayed until, until the same say then when I left. Uh, so that's why I didn't think that, yeah alternately so if he'd be able to take my empty flat if he stayed in town. But I have no idea why he, he left or what day it was or something like that.

EO: And so you left, and, after leaving you had contact with him then or with Anna?

JW: [inaudible]

EO: ... or with Anna?

JW: No, I, uh, however got a call from Donald Boström. When I was, when I was out of the country. Uh ... What day can that have been. Can't, can't really remember what day it was. But at any rate I got a call where, where he said to me, uh, are you sitting down. And, and I immediately became very worried. And so he said that, that Julian has been accused of rape, uh, of this younger girl Sofia. And that he had spoken with Anna Ardin. And that Sofia had spoken with, with him. And that Anna was royally pissed about uh, about what she heard from Sofia. Uh, and that she for one reason or another uh, had believed what Sofia told her. Uh, and that they would, would meet. Yeah now what day was that.

EO: And how, what happened after that with this information?

JW: Yeah I, I was totally in shock, uh ... What, what can one do with information like this like.

EO: No. Did you contact anyone or did anyone keep you informed of what was happening or?

JW: No in other words it was, it was during the day that I, that I still got, uh, had contact uh, with, uh, through Donald Boström. And, and then I went out into the country like I was, I was, yeah ... Has nothing to do with the interrogation but I was in Kazakhstan.

EO: Hmmm.

JW: And out on the Aral Sea, with very sporadic phone contact and Internet connectivity like and ... And everything it can be. Uh ... So I, I was totally in shock. And then the following day ... Yeah that's how it was, the day, the following day this came out as big headlines in, in the world media. And then a few hours later the whole thing, the whole thing was dismissed. Uh, and, for my, yeah first it was a total shock and, about it being an accusation and then it was a total shock about, uh, the story getting out so fast and the prosecutor grabbing onto it so fast. And then a total shock about, about the whole case being dismissed. Uh, so from my point of view, I only thought that this, it smelled completely wrong all of it from beginning to end. Because there was something there that didn't add up.

EO: And you followed the developments on the web or on ...

JW: Yeah, I got some calls ...

EO: OK.

JW: Uh, from Donald Boström. And of course I ... No I actually didn't have much time to follow it on the web. Uh ... There were a few times when I was able to connect to a network.

EO: Have you had any contact with Anna Ardin after ...

JW: I rang her the same day that, uh, that is precisely, the call after, after Donald Boström. But it was a short call, she was leaving to meet uh, Sofia to, uh, to go consult with uh, with the police. But what I learned from that call was that uh, I may have misunderstood but what I learned from that call it wasn't what, what Donald Boström had already told me. Uh but it was very simply that Sofia wanted to force Julian to ... Precisely, it, it's part of what I forgot. She wanted to force him to, uh, test himself. Uh, but not a police complaint of rape. Uh ... And that's what I learned from that conversation.

EO: And the test was for?

JW: HIV. In other words they were, as I understood it so they'd, uh, they'd had sex without, without ... But this is second hand sources from my side of things, it's what Donald Boström told me. That, and Anna. That they'd had sex without, without a condom. And that, uh, Sofia was afraid, afraid she'd been infected. And that she evidently had wanted to, to have Julian test himself. And Julian evidently didn't want to do that. Uh, precisely, then, then I actually spoke even with, with Julian. I rang him. Uh the time, the time frames like move into one another so it's difficult to remember the exact sequence of events.

EO: Hmmm, hmmm.

JW: But so I ring him and ask, what the fuck is going on. And then he says that yeah, what do you say, she wants me to, to test myself. So then fucking do it like. What, what's the problem. So, no but I, I can test myself but I don't want to be blackmailed to test myself. Um ... Because they say that either they go to the police, or, Sofia, that she either goes to the police or so I test myself. So I can give, I can give her that but I'd rather do it out of, out of, uh goodwill like rather than it's a blackmailing situation. I said, but fuck see you fucking test yourself now like. That's that, in other words if she's uneasy about it, it's crazy. Uh, and after that I didn't butt in, uh. And remember I'm 4500 kilometres like from a telephone ...

114

EO: Hmmm.

JW: And I have my head full of a lot of other things.

EO: But does he, does he say anything more about the relationship, in other words about his contact?

JW: Uh no, I think he may have said that he, that he had uh, had sex with, with Sofia. Um ... Don't think there was anything else he mentioned then.

EO: You didn't talk about Anna?

JW: No. Uh, other than that, uh Sofia was in contact with Anna. And that Sofia was very angry on Ann ... For, sorry, Anna was very angry on Sofia's account. I got the impression from that conversation that I had with Anna what Sofia, that Anna had, uh ... Had some sort of sisterhood feeling for the younger girl, that she wanted to help her. And as I understood it, that was why she was going to go with her to the police to get advice about how to force uh, Julian to uh, test himself.

EO: Did you ever get an idea of Julian's attitude towards women in general?

JW: Women in general. That's just as difficult a question as asking about Anna's attitude towards men in general.

EO: OK but I was thinking if he'd expressed something you reacted to or if he in some way showed ...

JW: No, I can instead say it's like I said, that during the two weeks I was with him he is an awful chick magnet.

EO: Hmmm ...

JW: But more from a very gentlemanly way with women. And later I understood afterwards, putting one and one together, that it was

115

probably a lot of girls who did everything they could to get into bed with him. And I don't know where they ended up but now it sounds like it can be a real lot who succeeded. But I didn't see anything unusual in his attitude towards them.

EO: No.

JW: But on the other hand as I said, there's a strange attitude towards men with Anna Ardin and her friends. And that's what I brought up with this ...

EO: Yes precisely.

JW: This little anecdote. But it was a feeling that kept on all evening from some of the girls at the crayfish party.

EO: Hmmm. Can I take a short pause in the interrogation. The time is 11 ... 10:55.

EO: So we can resume the interrogation 10:59. So, then we'll return to where we were and that was, you were talking specifically about Anna's friends' attitude to men rather than Julian's.

JW: Yes.

EO: OK.

JW: And as I said, I got a little, little weird vibes. This happens now and then especially in the universities, you run into something that ... I really don't know how to express this because it's coming out sooner or later in the evening tabloids, but it happens, happens now and then that you run into young women who've taken ... They've completed a journey, there in the name of feminism so they tend to be just as chauvinistic as the most chauvinistic men can be, but on the feminist scale. And it often expresses itself that they, certain young women can then talk about men as sexual tools and that they're not needed for intellectual conversation. And that it's only men who, or only women who, need one another. So maybe it's more a thing for my generation, maybe you've never run into it, but I run into it quite often, above all in the universities.

And I got, got that feeling from some of Anna's friends. Uh, and when this conversation, this short interpolation came up so I got a quick feeling that, that, yeah, no in other words I don't want to say that Anna uh, was like that. But she, she affirmed that side of things with, uh, with this woman, with her friend. Um ... That's the only thing in terms of character, but I don't know about it, if it should fall, if the shadow should fall on Anna. It's hard to, hard to judge.

EO: A final question, have you, we've touched on it earlier also precisely that you've spoken with Julian about his sex life or his, his, maybe what he would prefer in terms of sex. And you said you talked about his sex life.

JW: Absolutely not.

EO: But in conclusion then, have you at any time spoken about something, something in his private life as regards the sexual part, his preferences or what he likes in any way?

JW: Absolutely not.

EO: [inaudible] Nothing, nothing. Uh, has he ever ... Do you know if he has any children?

JW: Well I've read in the newspapers the same way as [inaudible].

EO: OK, But this was nothing you talked about or?

JW: As I said, my relationship with Julian ... So I understand after this interrogation, particularly considering it's about crayfish and things like that so it can seem we had a close private relationship but we actually have a professional relationship. And that, to be honest it doesn't interest me at all.

EO: No. Has he said anything about children or his, his wanting children here in Sweden?

JW: No, I haven't, haven't heard that. (Laughs.)

EO: No. OK, I'm satisfied. So you have any further questions, Mats?

MG: Yes some clarifications actually.

EO: Hmmm, hmmm.

MG: You said, was the first time you met Julian, it was in London?

JW: It wasn't the first time I'd met him but it was the first time in this, uh, during this period. Uh, I have, uh, even written about, about WikiLeaks previously, uh, and I've met him in New York. You can read about that in *Aftonbladet*.

MG: But approximately had you, like not known, but had contact if you say the first time you had any contact with him?
JW: Uh I'd met him in New York in, uh, April or something like that.

MG: Hmmm.

JW: And we've had, uh, some sort of, um, sporadic contact via email since then.

EO: Hmmm.

MG: Hmmm. We've talked about, concentrated a lot on the girls, how they behaved around, around him. That it was, as you yourself described it a bit groupies.

JW: Hmmm.

MG: A question I have, in other words how, in other words Julian, how he responded to this, this attention from the girls?

JW: I think that he ... Uh, that he thought it was nice. Uh, and what I think, as I said it was as I described it, it was why I had that talk with him. That it can seem as nice as anything but you have no idea who they are.

MG: At this crayfish party so you said that there were a lot of other girls, amongst others this girl who said something that, that you reacted to. Did any of these other girls try to get Julian's attention?

JW: That evening?

MG: Hmmm.

JW: Not in, in that way, uh ... Not in a physical way, I can put it like that. But, but, uh ... In other words if you imagine that there's a, a very famous rock star sitting at a party so there's going to be some looks and, and certain ways to, to more or less direct attention to one person. In that way I'd say that, that probably all the girls at that crayfish party behaved towards him. But no it wasn't sexual [inaudible].

MG: No. Julian himself at this crayfish party, did you notice if he made any overtures, not of a sexual, but in other words that he tried to get their attention?

JW: I don't notice that. Uh and, in other words it's about somewhere if, I don't know if you've met him yet but, uh ... Julian is a, a person who has certain character traits, uh, who, who like somewhere it, it, it ... I get the impression that he's a person who thinks it's, uh, that it's more stimulating for him to talk about his, his profession. In other words almost so it becomes an extreme situation. In other words you know, there are some people who, who can't distinguish like, or who on the contrary can distinguish between their professional and private lives. But Julian in my opinion is a person who is constantly interested by, by issues about politics and journalism uh and it shows as well in that regard in, in, uh, in his body language. That, uh, if you

119

think about looks like and, and overtures so it's more like looks and interest about an interesting topic of conversation.

MG: Hmmm.

JW: And it could be that it's a girl who starts an interesting topic of conversation, but I get that look from him too. But not a sexual look.

MG: No. OK. Do you know if ... No we'll drop that question. On the other hand you, we mentioned that you'd spoken with Anna about this cashmere girl.

JW: That's Sofia, the cashmere girl.

MG: The cashmere girl. But how, in other words it sounds, I get the impression that it's a bit derogatory.

JW: From Anna?

MG: Yes or from the both of you in that conversation about her, yeah like who is it.

JW: Yeah in other words, because she came from nowhere and there was no one who knew who, who, who she was. And it, in terms of appearance, it was a girl who, who did everything to play on her sexuality in a context where, where people were exceptionally professional. In their behaviour, then it turns out that people aren't always so professional like in other ways and it ... In other words from what you bring up here so it's demonstrated that Julian's obviously had sex with people. But, uh, in her behaviour she was definitely ... She didn't belong like.

MG: No. And that, that impression you think Anna also had?

JW: Yes from the SMS messages I read up for you too.

MG: Yeah, yeah.

EO: May I just ask, Sofia did you meet her that day?

120

JW: I met her that day.
EO: Any further questions?

JW: Uh ... No.

MG: And no contact either with her?

JW: (Inaudible.)

MG: No. OK. I have no further questions.

EO: Do you have any questions?

JW: [inaudible]

EO: No. So we conclude the interrogation at 11:10.

---

[1] See http://lawline.se/answers/3119.

[2] A former Israeli nuclear technician who revealed details of Israel's nuclear weapons programme to the British press in 1986 and was subsequently seduced during his travels by a female agent from Mossad and kidnapped back to Israel in the quintessential 'honey trap'.

[3] Sofia is reportedly 26 years old at the time of this meeting.

[4] Sofia is reportedly 26 years old at the time of this meeting.

[5] Sofia is reportedly 26 years old at the time of this meeting.

CHAPTER 9:

THE INTERROGATION OF DONALD BOSTRÖM

MONDAY 20 SEPTEMBER 2010

THE INTERROGATION OF DONALD BOSTRÖM

The interrogation of Donald Boström was conducted by Mats Gehlin with Ewa Olofsson as police interrogation witness on 20 September (31 days after the case was filed) starting at 11:20 and concluding at 12:17, immediately following the interrogation of Johannes Wahlström.

Donald Boström, author and photographer by profession, was in the Middle East researching a new book when members of the UN forces approached him to help investigate what appeared to be trafficking in body parts by Israeli forces. Boström filed his story, asking for a full investigation, with DN.se in Stockholm. DN.se, owned by the powerful Bonnier family, refused to publish the article. Boström then turned to Aftonbladet who agreed to publish, and a diplomatic crisis between Israel and Sweden ensued.

Although not a member of a political organisation like Anna Ardin, Boström was nevertheless asked by Ardin to assume her responsibilities with regards to Julian Assange for the time 11-14 August 2010, when she would be out of town.

Boström was to play a pivotal role in the events that led up to the incident at the Klara police station 20 August 2010. As was the case for Julian Assange and Johannes Wahlström, this was an audio-recorded interrogation that was later transcribed.

Signed by:	
Police authority:	Stockholm municipality
Date signed:	
Unit:	1KU/F Domestic violence group
Journal #:	0201- K246336-10
Interrogated:	Boström, Carl Donald
The interrogated is:	Witness
Civil registration #:	
Identify confirmed:	No
Relation to the suspect - complainant - witness:	
Interpreter:	
Language:	
Suspected crime / reason for interrogation:	Witness interrogation for the cases K 246314-10 and K 246336-10.
Advised of suspicion:	
Advised of right to attorney:	
Defender/representative is desired:	
Defender/representative is present:	
Accepts defender provided by the court:	
Chief interrogator:	Mats Gehlin
Date:	2010-09-20
Interrogation commenced:	11:20
Interrogation concluded:	12:17
Place of interrogation:	City police, Bergsgatan 48, Stockholm
Type of interrogation:	RB 23:6[1]
Method of interrogation:	Audio tape recording
Interrogation witness:	Olofsson, Ewa
Transcribed by:	JW

MG: Yes this is a little bit about your contacts with Julian Assange.

DB: Yup.

MG: To start with I'd like you to tell us how you got to know Julian and when you met him the first time.

DB: I met Julian the first time this spring, the spring of 2010, I don't remember exactly which month but it was in conjunction with his being interviewed by *Aftonbladet* by the journalist Johannes Wahlström. Ehee Ha [*sic*] and then I found out through Johannes and *Aftonbladet* that Julian was coming to Sweden and I was asked if I wanted to be in on a meeting.

EO: [inaudible].

MG: We'll do this anyway because it's still recording anyway.

DB: Otherwise I have one you can borrow.

EO: No it's something that ...

MG: But it's working.

DB: The batteries might be running low.

(Used two dictaphones for safety's sake.)

DB: Yeah.

EO: So.

MG: It can toot all it wants now.

DB: Yes.

MG: So, if you continue with ...

DB: With where I was.

MG: Yes.

DB: So Julian had a rather big presentation in Sweden through a big assignment, an interview in *Aftonbladet*. Uh, that was possibly what got him to decide to travel to Sweden, at that time. Then it turned out he had thoughts about Sweden anyway, in terms of freedom of expression and freedom of the press, in other words the legislation ... Uh, in connection with his coming here I was asked if I wanted to be in on a meeting ...

(One dictaphone stops working. The interrogation continues with only Olofsson's dictaphone.)

EO: It just died.

MG: We'll keep going with yours.

EO: So.

DB: With Julian and some journalists. And of course I said yes, I as many others was both curious and interested in what that was. Uh so we had a meeting, uh, with him, a number of journalists who had also been asked. What's happening now is that around WikiLeaks there's been a cooperation with journalists. Even newspapers and television corporations are involved. And in Sweden it was some sort of, embryo, it could have become the same thing. Uh, a number of journalists from different places of work but also *SVT* and *Aftonbladet* and media organisations too, also involved in these discussions. Uh, so of course it was very interesting.

Then Julian left the country again and came back one more time. And then we had another meeting, continued the discussion. If we're going to do this, we talked about, what should we do and how should we do it and what will we do. Uh, I remember it as, no decisions were made, no organisations were formed ... In other words nothing formal but there were like discussions. Uh but I remember approximately that all the Swedish journalists thought the same thing, that we look at these materials which are worth gold for a journalist of course, that we want the papers on the table. Here there was like the opportunity to get, literally, the papers on the table. For a lot of things, not just the known ones. Uh, and that we'd do it as journalists, make an assessment of public interest. And from that perspective, uh, publish, possibly publish something then. That's to say, not do as WikiLeaks normally do, publish everything. But we as a more, yeah a Swedish normal publicity angle on it. And we were mostly in agreement on that.

Uh, and then nothing more happened, then Julian left the country again. Uh and so this *Der Spiegel*, *New York Times*, *Guardian* joint venture happened. Uh, another venture's been planned, I know, where I'm not at all involved but ... Uh but approximately the same media are sitting and looking at materials. And we started talking about, uh, if we could have a similar project in Sweden with other materials. And where *Aftonbladet*, *SVT*, and a few, yeah other journalists were mentioned. It never happened, in other words any documents to look at, to dig into, researching has never manifested itself, uh, yet. But it's still in the air. After this storm has subsided so maybe it'll resume, maybe not. Uh, so on three occasions when Julian was in Sweden I've met him. And discussed these things, with a lot of others.

MG: The first time was in the spring?

DB: Yes, in the spring.

MG: Yeah, OK.

DB: And the second time was also before the summer.

MG: Yes. And this third time this is when he gives the lecture or?

DB: Precisely, in connection with the invitation from the Brotherhood movement. Uh, and then in conjunction with this Anna Ardin who've I not met rings me then but I got a good contact with her rather quickly. Uh, because there was an enormous media interest and she wondered if she could have me take care of the media coordination, at any rate a lot of media so that ... So when they rang her which is a part and inviting organisation so she bounced them most often onto me.

MG: OK.

DB: Uh so suddenly it became ... And I said, I've got more media experience than she does. Know a lot of these journalists who are ringing. So I said yes, I can do that without having any clue what enormous time it'd take. And suddenly a lot of people believe I'm some sort of media coordinator for WikiLeaks but that's not the way it was.

MG: No.

DB: I only helped out, helped Anna and the Brotherhood run this up until the conference. (Laughs.)

MG: Hmmm.

EO: Are you an active member of the Brotherhood ...

DB: No.
EO: Movement? No.

DB: No, no not at all.

MG: But you said Anna contacted you?

DB: Yes.

MG: Yes.

DB: Uh, I'd had contact with Peter Weiderud. I'd known him for years, or known, run into each other in international situations. Mostly I'm a foreign correspondent.

MG: Hmmm.

DB: Peter Weiderud at the Brotherhood, who's chairman of the Brotherhood is also very involved internationally so we've met sometimes in the parliament or yeah like that. Uh, but when this gig was to take place so Anna was given the assignment of being press secretary and then, then she rang me and asked, can you, can I shift a bit of media work to you. (Laughs.) I told her she could do that. And then a rather big circus started around this interest before the seminar. Uh, and then a new circus started a week later when Anna and the other women went to you. And then, then my telephone number was already on record with the world media so then came the next storm.

MG: OK.

DB: Uh ...

MG: Yes. During, if we say like this, when it all starts, these allegations ...

DB: Hmmm.

MG: What reaction, in other words if we say it like this, what reaction did you get from Julian then? Was it him, you have contact with him as I understand it?

DB: Yeah, I have, there's a background story beforehand in other words ... I had daily contact with Anna and Julian, in connection with the seminar. And Anna and I both had contact several times a day most often. Uh of course, because the media, that was a media turbo so we had a lot of contact.

And before this all starts Anna rings me and says like this, what I said before isn't true, we've actually had sex, Julian and me. Previously she said that they hadn't had it in other words spontaneously without anybody asking so she's joked about Julian living in her flat and sleeping in her bed but we haven't had sex. Of course he tried, she says but she's rebuffed him. Yeah no comments but we keep on joking.

But so the phone rings one day, I think it was Thursday then. Uh and I can hear in her voice that she, that it's something serious. So she says, it's not true what I said, we have too had sex. Aha, I say, I'm a little surprised she rings me and tells me this. Uh and then, and then she goes on to tell me that the other woman, Sofia has rung her and told her Julian was there and had sex with her. Both times it was consensual. And now I'm speaking as Anna, and this is the only version I have actually. Uh and we talked a lot, and I'm telling you all this to get back to your question ...

MG: Hmmm.

DB: Uh, because there's a background story. And then she tells me that Julian and Sofia travelled to Enköping and had consensual sex or however you say that, uh, up until the morning and then Anna says and then Sofia tells me Julian continues having sex with her in the morning without protection, without a condom. And she doesn't want that and she protests, uh, but Julian continues and completes the sex without protection despite Sofia's protests, says Anna. Uh, OK I say, I'm speechless of course from suddenly getting this call. And so I have to say that he, we had sex at an early stage at my place too and right in the middle, in an ongoing act or whatever he broke the condom, she says. She doesn't say, takes it off or she says ... For I get stuck with, breaking it, it's such a strange ... Either you have a condom or you don't, or so one takes, yeah ...

So therefore I remember exactly this description and she says to me that suddenly he breaks it, the condom, and continues against my wishes. Uh, and I was again unbelievably stupefied and couldn't comment, I was just a bit shocked of course about this happening.

So that's the background story and I believe, I think Anna is very, very credible. Or at least I've thought so all along. Uh, so I don't dismiss it but contact Julian and confront him with this right away. Something like what the fuck is going on? Um, and his reaction is shock, he doesn't understand anything, of course he has a contrary story. He says Sofia didn't protest at all, they were just having fun. Uh he, he, I really try to pressure him, did you take the condom off, did you break the condom, Uh, he doesn't even understand the question. So it's two separate, and I have no conclusions to draw from this ...

MG: No.

DB: At all. But that's the background story, and therefore I know, uh, what's coming so to speak. Because then Anna says Sofia's asked me to go to the police, follow along with her and I've decided I'm going to follow along and support her through this. But we're not going to file a complaint against Julian, we just want to go there and tell our stories. And so I wonder, can you tell a story without it becoming a complaint ... Yeah, technicalities like that but I'm not good at them, but that's what she says.

And so she goes there and follows along with Sofia. And we ring a few times back and forth, we send SMS messages a bit about this. And I ring as well and contact Julian a few times. Uh, they want Julian to test himself for HIV, uh, otherwise they're going to file a complaint. That's how they express it. Uh, they don't want to speak with Julian themselves. But Julian's talking to Sofia he says and he thinks things are blown out of proportion. But I tell Julian that, the girls want you to test yourself and if you do it, they won't file a complaint but if you don't, they'll file a complaint. So I just conveyed that, I was the messenger. I didn't have any of my own, uh, and that's the way it is.

And then Anna rings again and says now we've been with the police and Sofia told her story and, yeah because I sat there so I added a comment of my own. This is very 'word for word' and as I remember her telling me. Uh, aha I say, and what was that comment. Yeah that comment was that I think Sofia is telling the truth because I experienced something similar Anna says then. And then she told me that bit about the condom then, so that's why I think it's true. And I don't know anything about police technicalities but then Anna says, because we suddenly were two women who had a statement about, about the same man so it became a crime against the state and so it became a complaint even though we didn't file a complaint. And, yeah so it became a complaint. And I therefore already knew Julian's reaction, and now we're up to your question.

MG: Yes yes.

DB: Uh, that he was in shock and didn't understand anything. That was his first, uh … And, so that then there were two versions, first there was no sex uh, then there was sex but nothing had happened that Anna didn't want to happen. Uh, and then the third version now is that it's rape even. So I have, from my point of view I have seen three versions of the same incident.

MG: If we say, you've then, Julian has been here earlier. Have you, have you any insight or knowledge of his activities with women?

DB: Uh, yeah insight, we've never spoken privately and we've never associated privately.

MG: No.

DB: So precisely what he's done and with whom I don't know, but there's a common perception …

MG: Hmmm.

DB: Of course and it's that he attracts a lot of women. In other words it's so remarkable. And it's a little bit, yeah it's a bit of a rock star phenomenon so to speak.

MG: OK.

DB: The world's most famous man …

MG: Yes.

DB: In the eyes of some people, in other words during a certain period he was that. Unbelievably intelligent, that's attractive and he challenges, in other words the Pentagon and so ... That impresses a lot of people and I've seen very many women, I can say the overwhelming majority of women who've come into contact with him have fallen head over heels.

MG: Hmmm.

DB: Uh, they're totally enchanted. Uh, really. And I've been able to draw the conclusion that he's been able to take advantage of this, we can put it like that. But precisely with whom, how many and what, that I don't know.

MG: No. He, you get, in other words his, his reaction if one says ...

DB: Hmmm.

MG: What does he feel about this attention from the girls?

DB: I think he feels positively about it actually.

MG: Hmmm.

DB: One can, I understand the question but I think that he thinks it's positive and Anna's comments when she actually rings me and says, it wasn't true, what I said before, we've had sex.

MG: Hmmm.

DB: And then she adds that, right on this theme as I say, uh, I was fucking proud, got the world's coolest guy in my bed and living in my flat.

MG: Hmmm.

DB: Uh, yeah and it's on that theme and that was why, to your question now so it's, so I believe Julian thinks this attention is positive, very positive.

MG: Hmmm. The events surrounding Julian living with Anna ...

DB: Yes.

MG: Do you know about that?

DB: Yes. I was going to say, I'm the one who knows about that. Because that was when, for Julian's arrival that Anna rings me for the first time. And it's not a media matter but the fact that we've never spoken but, hi I'm Anna Ardin I have, so, I'm involved with, planning this seminar. I'll be on the election campaign trail so my flat will be empty, so Julian's welcome to live there she says, you can tell him that. Uh, and in addition the Brotherhood would earn, or save hotel costs. And Julian would rather live in a flat than in a hotel so I forwarded the message and he jumped on it and so I brought the two of them together, easy as that.

So that, and then it was the plan Julian would stay until Friday I think. The seminar would be on Saturday, Anna'd come home on Saturday I think it was originally. But then she comes back on Friday instead. So, and it's a little bit like this, wow how is this going to work, where's Julian going to spend the night and like that. Uh, but what I understand then, it's that they go out and eat, then they go home, uh, and they decide that Julian can stay in her bed. So that was the easy part, that Anna clearly understands, my flat is empty, it can be used. And she offers it to Julian, then he lives there for, for one more week.

MG: Yes. Do you have any contact with Julian this week then?

DB: Yes.

MG: After the seminar so to speak.

DB: Yes. Yes firstly so, after the seminar we go, then it's a Saturday. They met on a Friday and the seminar was on Saturday. So we go eat lunch, this is something I believe has been in the media. It's a little gang that lingers, when all the journalists have dropped out so there's only a few left. And there's also a woman standing there that I've seen during the seminar, whom I don't know and I don't know who she is. So polite as I am I say hello to her and ask, are you also a Brotherhooder like that. No not at all she says, uh, I just asked if I could help out. Uh, and then I understand that it's one of those, you can call them groupies or stalkers or those who are attracted by his starshine.

MG: Hmmm.

DB: But, yeah there's nothing more with that and she follows along and eats lunch with us.

MG: Who sees to it she follows along to eat lunch?

DB: Yeah, good question, but it's like this, Brotherhood says like this, lunch is on us, thanks for the seminar and now we'll go and sit down and eat lunch and she's sitting there.

MG: So you don't even know if she's been invited?

DB: No in other words she says like this, I rang Anna and asked if I could help out. So there was some sort of acceptance from Anna that she was there, got to join the gang. What she helped out with, I don't know but there was an acceptance that she was with us.

MG: Hmmm.

DB: Uh precisely, so she not only pushed her way in but she also ... Then, I'm the one who finishes lunch and leaves first for I have somewhere else to go. But before that Peter Weiderud says, because it's been in the media, that it's crayfish season and Julian from outside the country is here, it's crayfish season, uh, so he should, he should get to try Swedish crayfish. And so Anna starts ringing, this is a Saturday, after the seminar, so Anna rings some friends and says yep of course we're going to organise a crayfish party for Julian. And so she rings and delegates assignments, can you buy this and can you buy that. That's about the last thing I hear before I leave the restaurant and thank them and go on.

MG: Hmmm.

DB: And then it's, uh, a crayfish party in the evening, around 19:00 then.

MG: How were you invited, were you invited already at lunch ...

DB: Yes precisely, it's then, then I was invited. And it's, it's not a big party, it's a smaller party, um ... Amongst others it's two people from the Pirate Party who come that Anna's contacted. For the idea was Julian was to start living with them instead. Uh, so that's why they come so they can meet, be introduced. And then a few friends of Anna's too as well, uh, yeah.

MG: If we back up a bit to the lunch and that bit about Sofia who tags along.

DB: Hmmm.

MG: What did you think of Sofia's behaviour at the lunch restaurant?

DB: Uh I found her spec ... As, yeah my best expression for this is 'odd'. Uh, she said in essence nothing at all I don't think. Uh, she said that, precisely this bit that I rang Anna and asked if I could help out and then she said at one point that she worked at the natural history museum. That was what I heard her say, and ... So I didn't bother thinking much about her but, if you ask then yes, as an odd person.

MG: Did she speak with Julian at the lunch?

DB: Yeah they sat next to each other, uh, and they said something to each other and did something with each other but there I have no details.

MG: No.

DB: Uh, actually. Uh, the only thing one remembers, there's a person who fancies Julian.

MG: Hmmm.

DB: And as stated, Julian finds that positive. That's the impression and after that I don't delve into people's private lives like that ... But, but, yeah apropos that there's another detail too, that I thought of. That was, we were talking, I talked with Anna all the time.

MG: Hmmm.

DB: And she jokes about Julian, she says he's a special bloke. Suddenly he's just gone in the middle of the night and there he is sitting in the bathroom with his computer and ... Uh, she's joking rather wildly in a fun way about that. And, and we, sometimes so, tell similar stories. But at the crayfish party uh, so she's sitting next to Julian and then she says, and so she brings it up, where did you go off to last night she says. Uh, in other words, and I have no recollection they had any relationship at all. I really believe that Anna, that's a strong woman, [inaudible] like that so that ... Uh, but he catches on and he looks at her. Because I'm sitting right next to them. And, I woke up and you were gone from my bed and I felt like you'd dumped me she said. And precisely that word got me to jump. Uh, why did she feel dumped if she hadn't, yeah ... Uh, and I noticed afterwards now that I, that word came back that, that she ...

MG: But was that the night before the seminar in other words?

DB: No, it was after the seminar. Yeah yeah, right, the Friday night towards Saturday.

MG: Hmmm.

DB: That was when Julian was supposed to move but instead they went out and ate dinner, came back again, decided he'd stay on. And so they shared the bed. And then she told me with a laugh how he, weird guy who disappears and sits in the bathroom with his computer. But towards him there was another sentiment, that she felt dumped. And that's what I reacted to, because you don't do that if you don't have a relationship or like that, right. And what I knew they had no relationship, so that, wow she feels dumped, yeah ... Uh, that was during the crayfish party and so they sat and talked quietly about it for a while then, because it ...

Right and then she joked about Julian also disappearing with a 'random girl' according to the media. Because the ones who rang her uh, they asked for Julian and so, no but he disappeared with a 'random girl' and I didn't understand what she was getting at. And she meant after the lunch, which we've just talked about, Julian and Sofia went off to amongst other things the museum and the cinema and like that. But he came back for the crayfish party.

MG: During the crayfish party, is there anything more that happens that you pick up on during the crayfish party?

DB: Well, the only possibly relevant ... I can say I don't participate very much, I eat mostly, I love crayfish. (Laughs.) So I devote a lot of time to eating. But, uh, I know that they're talking about where Julian is going to sleep. Should he go back with this couple as planned. There's another one of Anna's friends, uh, and there's Anna. Uh, but I manage to understand it's already decided at the table Julian's going to stay with Anna again that night. Uh, without being a part of the discussion I understand that's how it's going to be, so that ... Again so I'm one of the ones who left the earliest. And the others are still sitting there and ...

MG: Si [*sic*] ...

DB: And then he goes up, then he and Anna go up and sleep there, what I heard anyway.

MG: Hmmm.

DB: I didn't see it. Maybe he did it in secret or how you want to put it, but it's nothing that I, like, saw him do.

MG: No.

DB: The classic, uh, yeah, man chases woman, in other words something like that ...

MG: No.

DB: No I, I remember that later he, and he wanted to keep seeing Anna. Because he said, no but I think it's best if I stay here afterwards. It's easiest, he found a formal reason like that, right. Instead of moving luggage and yeah ... So. So that was my impression. But I wasn't paying a lot of attention to those people. I, I know that I sat and ate more than what the others did. (Laughs.). Yeah.

MG: And then if we put it like this, Sofia, have you had any contact with Sofia, have you met Sofia other than at the lunch?

DB: No. That time was the last, time I ...

MG: And ...

DB: I haven't spoken with her, I haven't seen her.

MG: Did you beforehand, have any contact with Sofia beforehand?

DB: No. That was at the seminar there. I saw someone at the seminar who looked right special. In other words I noticed and but ... Everybody, everybody seemed to have a role there. There were journalists, there were technicians, and there were like organisers.

And she [*sic*] was very obvious that she didn't have a role. So I sat and thought but ... One thinks ... What can that be, can it be a member of the Pirate Party, can it be, yeah you know like that. And suddenly she was just standing there next to Julian like this, and yeah. That's why I introduced myself and then I understood OK it's one of, in the group of admirers so to speak.

MG: Then we return to, to this, a bit, that this bit about her living, about Julian living with Anna.

DB: Yes.

MG: And then, was it decided how long he would stay with Anna?

DB: No not what I know but he was actually to have moved on Friday as I said, was what, was what had been decided. And then he stays on and then I never heard that there was another limit. I haven't heard it. If they've talked about this together ... But I don't think so because, what you might want to arrive at is that gradually during that week, towards Wednesday and after that I think, so Anna says, I want him to move she tells me. Yeah but then tell him I tell her. And then she says it, yeah but I've told him she says but he doesn't want to move. And then I confronted him with that.

EO: Confronted Julian?

DB: Confronted Julian, the thing about moving, Anna says she wants you to move, she tells he she's asked you. And again he's surprised and says she hasn't said a word she says, he says.

MG: Hmmm.

DB: And again I can ... In other words I have ...

MG: Yeah.

DB: I get two, it's like stereo speakers, the one channel says one thing and the other says another thing. But never has there been mention of a time limit but a certain day no now I want you to move.
MG: Hmmm.

DB: She tells me. And I convey this to Julian, that's the situation. And it's first on Friday I believe, that he moves.

MG: Hmmm. Where does he move to?

DB: Good question. I don't know. I think you should ask Johann, maybe you have. Uh, I have not been involved in the arrangements for his accommodations. Not at any point. Uh, actually, and I have not been visiting him uh, even, where he moved to for example then. But my recollection is that it wasn't in Stock ... That the first stop was outside Stockholm somewhere. Uh, and now I know he's in Stockholm again but haven't been in the, uh, the place he lives now. Or ...

MG: No. Do you know, did anyone, did you hear Anna comment on Sofia or that in other words, did she bring up Sofia before this thing with the HIV tests and stuff like that? Did she mention Sofia at all?

DB: No the only thing, the only thing I heard that was what I said right now that she called her a 'random girl'.

MG: Hmmm.

DB: Uh, with, with a shrug of her shoulders or she like tried to joke about Julian disappearing with ...

MG: Hmmm.

DB: A 'random girl'. I didn't hear anything else.

MG: OK.

DB: Uh, you should maybe ask her girlfriends how she ...

MG: Yes.

DB: Those closest to her. No so it was rather apparent at the time that she gave the impression for me, in other words Anna held a style and a line with me that was pleasant, credible, straight, fresh in some way. But then what happened, I understood later that a lot of things had happened. That the impression wasn't correct ...

MG: No.

DB: Uh, corresponded with reality.

DL: No.

DB: So, hmmm.

MG: How, and then when this comes out ... In other words when she rings and tells you this ...

DB: Hmmm.

MG: About things having happened with Sofia.

DB: Yes.

MG: And that you, even then, she tells you what was true and like that.

DB: Yeah.

MG: What do you think about her when she tells you what she claims has happened?

DB: I find it, uh ... I was, partly I was of course flabbergasted that it's a completely different impression all of a sudden.

MG: Hmmm.

DB: Uh, but then I think that, that I think she's credible. And a bit like this, a woman who is in trouble you want to believe, in some way like that OK, it's like ...

MG: Hmmm.

DB: Uh, yeah so that was my feel, direct feeling.

MG: Hmmm.

DB: And yeah, but at the same time when, have, I got this thought, how could they have sex, consensual as she described it, so then something happens which she says is an assault, how could she gleefully arrange crayfish parties, let him go on living there, share her bed with him, and so forth. So I felt that here, here is something here that doesn't add up. So I had both the feeling of her as a credible person but that something nevertheless didn't add up in her story.

MG: No.

DB: But I decided not to dig into it, I won't dig into it, you get to do that right? (Laughs.)

MG: Yeah! (Laughs.)

DB: So that it's those two impressions I have in parallel, a credible girl, a strong girl who knows what she wants but something doesn't add up. And it's magnified a bit because I now have three versions of what happened.

MG: Hmmm.

DB: Uh, and Julian still says the same thing, I don't understand anything.

MG: No.

DB: They liked this a lot and they really wanted me, yeah. Uh, so that yeah ...

EO: Can I get a question in here?

MG: Of course.

EO: When you speak, when you spoke with Anna ...

DB: Hmmm.

EO: And she says she's been the victim of a sexual assault. Do you, do you get the feeling of what you thought she was subjected to actually, or Sofia?

DB: Yeah, uh ...

MG: Based on Anna's story.

DB: Yes, I understand. Based on Anna's story, when she rings me and says we had sex and this happened so she didn't at all imply she's been the victim of sexual assault. In other words she doesn't even want to go to the police. But, she expresses it like I want, I'll go along with, I promised Sofia I'd go along with her for support. Not that she had any business with the police herself. And so my impression is that she didn't experience anything serious but was mostly angry. As in don't fucking break the condoms but not that it was an assault. Uh, this is my impression because she doesn't go to the police for her own sake.

Then she rings back and says that, as stated what I said then that because she supported Sofia's story with that comment so the case turned out as she said, expressed it, stronger. She said precisely that.

EO: Hmmm.

DB: But it wasn't her case. Then if she went to you and presented her own case strongly, I don't know, but to me because that was the question.

EO: Yes, yes absolutely.

DB: So she trivialised it a lot as an unpleasant thing or something she got pissed about. Uh, and no plans to file a complaint or pursue it any further.

MG: But this is then before you, this is before it ... I feel it's like ...

DB: This is on Thursday, uh ...

MG: And when she goes to the police, do you know?

DB: Yeah, Friday, uh, I think she goes to the police. And on Saturday I think, uh, the arrest, Julian's arrested in absentia on Saturday. So that, yeah Friday afternoon Anna rings me rather often or we ring each other, a real lot, a real lot of times that Friday. And now, she says, now Sofia's with the police. Now I've been with the police and now it's HIV tests again and ... So on this Friday there's a lot of traffic, uh ... But she gives me the impression she's going there to say this. Uh, and she's a supportive friend for Sofia. Precisely ...

MG: What she ...

DB: Yeah.

MG: ...tells you, what do you think about that?

DB: Yeah, I figure it's just like that. Or believe her straight away.

MG: Hmmm.

DB: For when this gets out I know that I've spoken with, I get a call from *Aftonbladet*. And I decided I didn't want to speak to the media. I don't want to get pulled into this story. It's not my story so to speak.

147

MG: No.

DB: Uh, I haven't been in on these ... And like that, so that ... Uh but I know I tell *Aftonbladet* right away that I thought, what I told you, that Anna seems a credible girl. I remember I told *Aftonbladet* that.

MG: Hmmm.

DB: But then there's still those, things that don't add up in the story.

MG: Hmmm.

DB: But she, yeah ...

MG: Have you ever talked with Julian about, yeah, women? Have you ever talked with him, in other words ...

DB: Yeah, I understand the question, yeah.

MG: This about how they, how he gets swarmed all the time.

DB: Yeah, yeah.

MG: And have you had, yeah shall we say ethical conversations with him?

DB: Yes.

MG: You have?

DB: Yes, I have.

MG: Yes.

DB: Uh, because there's such an astonishing onslaught of women. In other words it takes seconds, in other words it's obvious ... And when it's like that so uh, so I think one has to um, keep things under control. For different reasons, in other words partly there's an ethical, moral way then so to speak but, but uh, I can't actually get into that for I don't know what he's done and not done so to speak what.

MG: No.

DB: It's like take care of ... It was like this, if it's going to be like this so one must, a, take care of it really, really well. Take care of it so no girls, yeah ... But the other thing we spoke about and got caught up in with our discussions that is more the security angle. Uh, that he's given the impression of himself, which I think is partly accurate at any rate, of being a hunted man. He's not really all too popular in the US. According to reliable sources that I've read in many places so over one hundred people, who they are in the Pentagon who are trying to crack his codes, yeah ... There's a hunt around, uh, and above all he's sitting on materials that can hurt, that they in the US think can hurt them.

MG: Hmmm.

DB: Uh, but not just the US. Iceland was the same and there are other countries.

MG: Hmmm.

DB: Uh, so, so they want, in other words it's an intelligence source that's unparalleled. That's why it's journalistically interesting in other words to see the papers on the table. So it's not difficult to draw the conclusion that there are a lot of people who want to stop him. Then I don't think there's anyone who wants to attack him physically, but they can do other kinds of things.

And even if it's conspiratorial so there are a lot of stories through history where they send out a girl in a short skirt. Uh, it wasn't so long ago in Russia, uh, you who are in that business know more about that than me. (Laughs.) Uh, editor-in-chief and journalists and it was only a few months ago, she filmed and taped it all. Uh, and we, we talked about that. And we also talked about uh, Vanunu the

Israeli scientist who exposed nuclear weapons in Israel. That was the same thing, they sent a girl to his hotel room so it was a done deal. Then they could smuggle him back to Israel and so forth.

So we talked about there being two sides to it, partly take care of things neatly with the girls. But, but he starts sailing up as a person who can qualify, become the victim for different ... Uh, yeah we talked about that, in those terms.

MG: Yeah and what does he say?

DB: Yeah, I only remember him saying that he understands.

MG: Yes.

DB: Uh, and yes that's the way it is but I also get the impression, don't remember the exact words, but my impression is still that he thinks he's in control. That he, because he understands it so he thinks about it and ...

MG: Yeah.

DB: The girls he meets are the ones he's learned to trust or not trust, is something ...

MG: But did you get ... From your, yes if one then, [inaudible] conspiratorial conversation you had with him.

DB: Hmmm.

MG: Do you feel, is there any reason to think in those terms in this case?

DB: I don't think so. Uh in other words no, if one now, one can think in different ways. That is if one should now think Pentagon and CIA and those types ...

MG: Hmmm.

150

DB: No I don't think so, I don't think that at all, no such conflict.

MG: Has Julian suggested it's something like that?

DB: No he hasn't. He, he's mentioned that it's a smear campaign. But he, he doesn't know where it's coming from. Or he can only corroborate the entire world media.

MG: Hmmm.

DB: Assange plus rape gets several million hits on the net. So it's a gigantic smear campaign he says but ... No I, I don't think he thinks it's the CIA behind it.

MG: Yeah or ...

DB: Or, this bit ... No, not in this case. But, but he's also said that he has, because he has leaks he's also had, uh, what's it called, information from an intelligence service that he has to be careful for they have seen indications that there are such plans underway.

MG: Hmmm.

DB: But not that this would be the plan, but in general. Uh, no so I can say that, here there's enough, yeah ... Then there are always things you don't know about and like that but, but ... If you only ask me like that, so no I don't think it's any big, I think it's more private, personal.

MG: Yes. You said that you'd confronted Julian as well in conjunction with, with your getting this from Anna.

DB: That's right.

MG: Did he say anything about what had happened? That is did he way that no, no but I don't understand anything ...

DB: Yes.

MG: But ...

DB: No.

MG: Did he elaborate by telling you what had happened?

DB: Yes a bit, that is it wasn't a lot but it was just to, I don't understand what you're talking about because, yeah we had sex precisely as usual.

MG: Hmmm.

DB: She, and I said as well like this that, Anna said that Sofia protested, clearly and loudly that, no don't go on.

MG: Hmmm.

DB: And then he became, he became upset several times. I've brought that up several times. And then he gets like upset, he absolutely didn't do that he says emphatically, or she didn't do that. And so he says as well that it's a pure, pure, pure, pure lie.

MG: Hmmm.

DB: And, and then he says only that, he had ordinary sex. And what leaked out to the media that we joked about what we'd name the baby and like that.

MG: Yeah.

DB: So that's well, more than that he didn't say but that we had sex and continued even though ...

MG: Did he say whether he had a condom or not?

DB: On that occasion with Sofia, no condom.

MG: Hmmm.

DB: Uh, on the other occasion, [inaudible] why the condom broke. And then, then he said no, he hadn't broken it. That is he meant that we continued as usual.

MG: But did you ...

EO: With or without a condom?

DB: As I understood it, with a condom. In other words it was protected sex on that occasion.

MG: Yes.

DB: Consensual protected sex and so he didn't at all break ... That's his version, to me.

MG: How, what do you know about Julian privately, in other words do you have any way to know what his life is like purely ... Is he married, does he have children?

DB: I know very little, I know some things that is but very, very little. Most of it comes from other newspaper articles.

MG: Hmmm.

DB: There are some people who've now tried to dig into his background. Uh, but I know very very, very little but I know that he, he has, he isn't married. And he has, I think at least four children I think. He doesn't talk much about his private life. Which is fine by me, I don't need to talk about things like that. That's not our role but ... And to my knowledge he has no residence, that is he has no permanent address but circulates around.

MG: Hmmm. Have you, has he ever expressed a desire to have more children?

DB: Uh not with me, that is we're talking about ... He's not a person who talks about his private life.

MG: No.

DB: He's very ... Uh, and as I said that's fine by me, I don't need ...

MG: Yup.

DB: Talk about it, so that no we haven't discussed that.

MG: No. Yes, Ewa?

EO: I see a few things here. Uh, yeah, had, had Julian anyone, did he talk about his future life like, did he want to establish himself here in Sweden or?

DB: Yeah right, hmmm.

EO: What were his thoughts?

DB: His idea as he expressed it to me or to others at any rate was to establish himself in Sweden. Apply for a work permit and a residence permit, which he's done.

EO: Hmmm.

DB: That is he's sent in the paperwork I know that. Uh and then go on to establish, uh, a publication in Sweden. Uh, and to do that get a publisher licence then, then be an official publisher. And thereby Sweden would be some sort of base for his life and activities. Uh, but no more details about how he'd live, I mean like that but this was a purely professional thought for the future. Work and residence permits, publisher licence, uh start a publication and Sweden would be some sort of main base for that activity. And that shows a direction forward in the future that is how he thinks. He yeah, his connections with Sweden would be strengthened and be more permanent and more ... And that's a clear impression I have.

EO: Hmmm.

DB: And, yes it's in that direction, that is he reckons on working to achieve that.

EO: Hmmm. Yes, precisely. I thought, do you still have contact with Anna?

DB: No. We had a little, I'll look when the last, that is right in the turbo we had contact a while afterwards. And then it was more and more seldom. I rang a few times, she didn't answer. And that was after Claes Borgström got in the picture. And my conclusion I think, because we had a good relationship. In one of the last, her last SMS message so she writes that we trust each other, right, so ... So my conclusion is that she's worried that I'm going to speak with the media or above all else *Aftonbladet*, because I have a lot of contact with *Aftonbladet*. And that therefore she reduces our communication so there are no leaks. I can imagine the solicitor says that, don't talk with any journalists even if they're friends. I'd namely say that. So that the last time she didn't answer, instead it's been some SMS messages and then ... Yeah since a bit more than a week or more she hasn't even sent an SMS message.

EO: Hmmm. And your contact with Julian these days?

DB: I haven't seen him in ten days or something like that, or met him. But we've spoken, yeah maybe four, three, four days ago. Uh, but it's actually, I want to say regularly, but irregularly, regularly. It's now and again like that.

EO: And because he knows, yeah because you've followed along, do you talk about his case very much, this ongoing preliminary investigation, does he touch on this, does he ask you things? Do you have a dialog ...

DB: Yes we do. But it's not so much dialog as it is more that he expresses his thoughts for example that nothing will happen before the elections. In other words an election tactic suddenly so to speak OK, that should it, if the case should go the one way or the other it'd hurt a party in the case that's on a parliamentary ballot, for example.

EO: Hmmm.

DB: Uh, I think he thinks about it a lot. And we don't talk very often, but the times we talk it comes up, this case comes up. He feels it clearly, yes he expresses [inaudible] discontent, he feels unjustly treated. For example a tangible thing that usually comes up, there was a murder case that was in the newspapers, Nancy in Malmö, a young girl who got chopped to death with a bottle I think. The individual is brought in, sentenced to eight years prison. The photo of the murderer is pixelated but the photo of Julian who is only a suspect is not pixelated. Uh, so that he feels there's something going on that's not right in general, and he comments on this often. But we've sat like this and like long, it's mostly phone conversations that are ... Yeah, and so forth in that way so to speak.

MG: Who in Sweden does he have the best contact with, Julian? Who would you say is the one he here in Sweden trusts the most?

DB: Yeah it's a bit here and there but if I were to name one person I'd probably say Johannes Wahlström. I think they made good contact in the US when Johannes interviewed Julian.

MG: Do you have any contact, how has your contact with Johannes looked from ...

DB: The beginning of time?

MG: Yeah or more correctly, no but if we say after the bomb was dropped.

DB: Yeah in principle Johannes has been out of the country all this time. Now I don't know if we've spoken by phone once or twice and a few SMS messages. That is it's been very little, low frequency contact.

MG: Hmmm.

DB: That is this is nothing we've ripped up and people have been running to meetings, sat and planned. But this is something that goes on as it goes on. And the last SMS message from Johannes was well, yeah yesterday. And I didn't reply, I didn't have the energy ... He can come to my place and have a look himself. (Laughs.) So it's on that level so to speak.

MG: Yeah.

DB: There are no, like, plans, there are no fractions like that but ...

MG: And before this? So did you know him a long time before this or?

DB: No. I've met him, um, once in Jerusalem on a common, a lot of journalists gathered. So that's why I knew who he was. Then he interviewed me once about the middle east for some magazine. Uh and that was the first time I met him and spoke with him. The third time I met him, the first time with Julian in principle, Assange.

MG: And where was this?

DB: I think, uh ... Let me think, I might be missing something here. Yes, I met him, I wrote, also. So if you write about the middle east you'll often get flak.

MG: Hmmm.

DB: A lot more. So suddenly I can say that, yeah I know him.

MG: Hmmm.

DB: But that's only recently that, that we've come that far.

JA: Yes.

EO: Hmmm. I have no further questions.

MG: Anything you think we should have asked that you want to get across?

DB: I think I've covered everything. No but there's this, it feels like, uh, there are so many versions of the same events.

MG: Hmmm.

DB: I think about that.

MG: Hmmm.

DB: And some people, Anna who's sitting and feeling dumped next to Julian. That too sticks in my ... Why felt that.

EO: One thing, when this phone call comes, on Thursday, when Anna ...

DB: Yes.

EO: And then you confronted Julian.

DB: Yes.

EO: Did it come out that he'd had sex with both Sofia and Anna or were you completely focused on Sofia?

DB: No in other words, when Anna rings, that is I think that's Thursday then.

EO: Hmmm.

DB: Up to then she's joked about, he hasn't got me between the sheets, and like that OK.

EO: Hmmm, hmmm.

DB: Uh, but Thursday then, that's when she says that, I've also had sex with Julian ...

EO: Hmmm ...

DB: What I told you before isn't true, so that's when it comes out that they've had sex.

EO: Hmmm ...

DB: And then the reason she says that, it's because Sofia rings her and tells her about their night ...

EO: Hmmm.

DB: So that within a few minutes I understand, everyone understands I almost said, so it came out that they'd both had sex with Julian. But to add: consensual sex.

EO: But then, you confront Julian with this.

DB: Yes.

EO: Is it also, do you also talk about both ...

DB: Yes.

EO: Girls?

DB: I told you explicitly what, precisely what Anna told me, I say that straight out.

EO: Yes.

DB: This broken condom and, why did you continue when Sofia said no, protested.

EO: Hmmm.

MG: Yeah then we come in inadvertently in this that, do you know if Julian has had any contact with the girls?

DB: No ...

MG: After ...

DB: Not after the complaint but that Friday, uh, when the girls actually go to the police [inaudible] I think it was a Friday. Before that Anna rings me frequently. Uh, and above all that we want him to test himself so then we won't file a complaint she says. OK I say, I'll ring Julian and tell him that. And so I do. And so I ring Anna and Anna rings me.

And then I ring Julian again and then he says, no but now I've had a long conversation with Sofia. He says on Friday. And she, [inaudible] no worries, that's to say she's not going to the police and that was, they were fully in agreement and ... I say, is it really true I say because Anna, when I spoke with Anna right now I got a completely different impression, they're on their way to the police [inaudible]. No he says, she, we were in complete agreement, it was very friendly, very nice.

And what he comes back to several times, and it's that I've spoken with her on Friday and she said like this. But after that I don't know if they've had any contact. But I don't think they've had any contact.

MG: Good.

EO: Hmmm. No ...

MG: Then we'll end the interrogation at 12:17.

---

[1] See http://lawline.se/answers/3119.

CHAPTER 10:
THE INTERROGATION OF JOAKIM WILÉN

WEDNESDAY 6 OCTOBER 2010

THE INTERROGATION OF JOAKIM WILÉN

The interrogation of Joakim Wilén, Sofia Wilén's younger brother, was conducted on the telephone by Mats Gehlin on 6 October 2010, 47 days after the case was filed, starting at 17:38 and concluding at 17:55 - seventeen minutes.

One typo in particular is retained in the translation for obvious reasons.

Signed by:	
Police authority:	Stockholm municipality
Date signed:	
Unit:	1KU/F Domestic violence group
Journal #:	0201-K246314-10
Interrogated:	Wilén, Kjäll Joakim
The interrogated is:	Witness
Civil registration #:	
Identify confirmed:	No
Relation to the suspect - complainant - witness:	Brother of complainant
Interpreter:	
Language:	
Suspected crime / reason for interrogation:	Interrogated as witness concerning his observations about the event
Advised of suspicion:	
Advised of right to attorney:	
Defender/representative is desired:	
Defender/representative is present:	
Accepts defender provided by the court:	
Chief interrogator:	Mats Gehlin
Date:	2010-10-06
Interrogation commenced:	17:38
Interrogation concluded:	17:55
Place of interrogation:	Telephone
Type of interrogation:	RB 23:6[1]
Method of interrogation:	Conceptual interrogation
Interrogation witness:	
Transcribed by:	

Joakim said he's the younger brother of Sofia. He said he knew of Sofia's interest in Wikileak [*sic*] and she thought they did a good job. She also thought Julian Assange was interesting because he represented Wikileak [*sic*]. Sofia told him that by pure coincidence she'd found Julian Assange was going to speak in Stockholm and that she had been given a seat for the lecture. Joakim said she thought it would be cool to hear what he had to say.

Joakim said the next time she met Sofia was a morning outside the ICA food store. It was approximately 08:00. Sofia was agitated and told him that there had been a problem with a cable and that she'd been to a party afterwards and that Julian Assange had followed her home. Sofia told him that Julian Assange was in her flat and that it felt strange. Joakim thought Sofia was a bit shook up by the situation. She asked Joakim if he wanted to meet Julian Assange but he didn't want to. He drove Sofia home and then went home to his own place.

The next time Joakim heard anything from Sofia was through an SMS message she sent him where it said Julian wasn't so nice. Joakim didn't learn what had happened until Sofia went to the police and one could read about it in the newspapers. He learned what had happened through Sofia and his mother. The latter said that Julian had had sex with Sofia without a condom and against her will whilst she was asleep.

Sofia has later said that she didn't want to file a complaint against Julian but only wanted him to test himself. She sought the police for advice and the police filed a complaint. Sofia also said she'd spoken with Julian about testing himself and Julian told her he didn't have time to test himself and she should take him at his word that he wasn't infected.

Joakim replied to a question from the chief interrogator that he and Sofia don't talk about sexual matters with each other.

Joakim said Sofia was mostly angry about what had happened and was sick from the inhibitor drugs she'd been given. She was also

165

upset that the incident had made it to the media and created such a stir.

Read back and approved.

---

[1] See http://lawline.se/answers/3119.

CHAPTER 11:

THE INTERROGATION OF SETH BENSON

FRIDAY 22 OCTOBER 2010

THE INTERROGATION OF SETH BENSON

The interrogation of Seth Benson, Sofia Wilén's former boyfriend from the US, was conducted on the telephone by Mats Gehlin on 22 October 2010 (68 days after the case was filed) starting at 14:15 concluding at 14:35 - twenty minutes.

Seth Benson was registered as living in the same flat as Sofia up to and including the time of Sofia's approach to Julian Assange, even though it's believed that by then he'd moved to Karlskrona (south of Stockholm) where he was enrolled at the rather exclusive (and expensive) Hyper Island media/PR institute.

Seth Benson was registered as living at that address for quite some time afterward, but today is again in the US. Shortly after the 'intermezzo', Sofia Wilén somehow got a new flat in the same area and formally moved to the new address. As of December 2010, there are no official records at all of Sofia Wilén's whereabouts. But Seth Benson was, despite working in Karlskrona, still registered at Sofia Wilén's old Enköping address until he left the country.

This interrogation was also a narrative-style 'conceptual interrogation'.

Signed by:	
Police authority:	Stockholm municipality
Date signed:	
Unit:	1KU/F Domestic violence group
Journal #:	0201-K246314-10
Interrogated:	Benson, Seth Ryan
The interrogated is:	Witness
Civil registration #:	
Identify confirmed:	No
Relation to the suspect - complainant - witness:	
Interpreter:	
Language:	
Suspected crime / reason for interrogation:	Interrogated as witness concerning his observations about Complainant 1
Advised of suspicion:	
Advised of right to attorney:	
Defender/representative is desired:	
Defender/representative is present:	
Accepts defender provided by the court:	
Chief interrogator:	Mats Gehlin
Date:	2010-10-22
Interrogation commenced:	14:15
Interrogation concluded:	14:35
Place of interrogation:	Telephone
Type of interrogation:	RB 23:6[1]
Method of interrogation:	Conceptual interrogation
Interrogation witness:	
Transcribed by:	

Seth said he had a relationship with Sofia for two and one half years. They lived together for the last year of this relationship. Seth said that for Sofia it was very important they always used condoms. Partly for the risk of infection and partly to avoid unwanted pregnancies.

Seth said the question of infection was a central one for Sofia and before they had sex the first time, they'd tested themselves and then read each other's test results. During the subsequent two and one half years they never had sex without a condom. This was completely unthinkable for Sofia. Seth said 'that was the agreement'. He said that what he knew, Sofia had never had sex with anyone without a condom.

Seth said he found out what happened when Sofia sent him an SMS message and asked if she could ring him. He was a little confused as they'd not had contact for several months. When Sofia rang she asked straight away what Seth thought of WikiLeaks and Julian Assange. He told her the WikiLeaks website seemed good.

Then Sofia said she'd been raped by Julian Assange by virtue of his initiating sex with her whilst she was asleep and not using a condom. Sofia told him she asked Assange if he was wearing anything. Assange was to have then answered 'yes - you'.

The chief interrogator asked Seth how Sofia reacted to this.

Seth said Sofia told him she'd been Shocked [*sic*] and not known what to do. Seth said that considering Sofia's determined opinion about condoms when having sex, he can imagine she was very shocked and very afraid. He knows how important it is for Sofia that condoms always be used when she's having sex.

Sofia told Seth that she couldn't understand how a representative of WikiLeaks who does so much good could have so little respect for another human being.

Read back and approved.

---

[1] See http://lawline.se/answers/3119.

CHAPTER 12:
THE INTERROGATION OF MARIE THORN

WEDNESDAY 27 OCTOBER 2010

THE INTERROGATION OF MARIE THORN

The interrogation of Marie Thorn, a work colleague of Sofia Wilén, was conducted on the telephone by Mats Gehlin on 27 October (68 days after the case was filed) starting at 17:00 and concluding at 17:25.

It may be inferred from the interrogation that Marie Thorn also lives in Enköping. There are however no records of anyone with her name in that area and in fact there is only one person in Sweden registered with the same name— but at an address south of Stockholm and perhaps two hours or more by public transport from Enköping.

As for most of the previous interrogations, this is a narrative-style 'conceptual interrogation'.

Signed by:	
Police authority:	Stockholm municipality
Date signed:	
Unit:	1KU/F Domestic violence group
Journal #:	0201-K246314-10
Interrogated:	Thorn, Marie
The interrogated is:	Witness
Civil registration #:	
Identify confirmed:	No
Relation to the suspect - complainant - witness:	
Interpreter:	
Language:	
Suspected crime / reason for interrogation:	Interrogated as witness concerning her observations about and conversations with Sofia.
Advised of suspicion:	
Advised of right to attorney:	
Defender/representative is desired:	
Defender/representative is present:	
Accepts defender provided by the court:	
Chief interrogator:	Mats Gehlin
Date:	2010-10-27
Interrogation commenced:	17:00
Interrogation concluded:	17:25
Place of interrogation:	Telephone
Type of interrogation:	RB 23:6[1]
Method of interrogation:	Conceptual interrogation
Interrogation witness:	
Transcribed by:	

Marie said she was a work colleague of Sofia's at the natural history museum where they both had hourly wages.

Sofia spoke some weeks earlier with Marie about her interest in wikileaks [*sic*] and Julian Assange. Sofia read a lot about the organisation on the Internet and she thought Julian Assange was very interesting as he seemed very intelligent and did good things.

Marie heard that Sofia got a seat at the lecture Julian was to hold in Stockholm. Sofia told her she'd mailed the arrangers and been granted admission. She was very excited and nervous before the lecture. Marie said they'd had contact on the day of the lecture. Sofia was happy and excited when she was on her way to the lecture.

Marie received several SMS messages from Sofia during the lecture, amongst other things that she was supposed to purchase a cable for Julian's computer and later that Sofia would be eating lunch with him. For example Marie received an SMS message that read: 'he looked at me'.

Later Marie learned that Sofia would be taking Julian to the museum where she worked in the information department. They arrived and Sofia borrowed Marie's badge. Marie discovered she needed the badge and went into the staff room where they were sitting. Julian sat and was surfing on the Internet and Sofia sat next to him. Then they went into Cosmonova to see the movie. When they came out after the movie Sofia told her she and Julian had been making out inside Cosmonova.

Marie said they had a lot of contact and she doesn't remember what was sent via SMS or if they spoke on the telephone. She knows Sofia was waiting for Julian on an occasion and that they travelled to Enköping. The night of the incident Marie was lying asleep and awakened when she received SMS messages from Sofia. What Marie remembers the contents weren't positive. That it had been bad sex, that Julian was nuts. That she has to go test herself because of his long foreplay. In the morning Marie recollects that they spoke with one another when Sofia was in the store to buy breakfast. Sofia was pissed that she had to buy everything and treat to breakfast as well as cater to him. She was bothered by him.

Marie didn't get to hear about the assault until the day after or if it was two days after and got the impression Sofia was very worried she could have been infected. Sofia told her then that she'd told Julian she could be pregnant so Julian said it was nothing to worry about and they'd name the child 'Afghanistan'. He'd pay off her student loans if she kept the baby.

They talked a bit when Sofia had gone to the police and the media blitz began. Sofia was very upset over the media attention and was mad with Julian. They spoke and sent SMS messages to each other. Marie doesn't remember directly what they said or wrote, but that they spoke about going to *Expressen*, this because Julian had spoken to *Aftonbladet*. This was only something they said and they had no intention of actually doing it. Marie has in any case not spoken with any newspaper.

Marie said Sofia had been contacted by a newspaper in the US and then Marie joked with Sofia about asking for a lot of money.

The chief interrogator asked about the SMS message when Marie wrote that they have to figure out a good plan of revenge.

Marie said that this wasn't something they planned to do either. It was more an expression for Sofia's frustration. Marie has tried to support and agree with Sofia in their conversations. She wanted to help Sofia in a difficult situation.

Marie also wants to point out that she's spoken so much with Sofia that it's difficult to remember what was said and what was not said. Marie wants to point out that when Sofia was at the hospital and went to the police, things didn't turn out as Sofia wanted. She only wanted Julian to test himself. She felt she'd been overrun by the police and others around her.

Read back and approved.

---

[1] See http://lawline.se/answers/3119.

CHAPTER 13:
THE LAB RESULTS

THE LAB RESULTS

These are the lab results presented to Chief Inspector Mats Gehlin on Monday 25 October 2010. At this point, only one interrogation remained (that of Marie Thorn).

Gehlin had submitted two condoms to the state crime lab SKL (Statens kriminaltekniska laboratorium, http://skl.polisen.se) on 25 August, exactly two months earlier, which was quite the feat, as one came from Sofia Wilén— even though Chief Inspector Eva Finné, who was in charge of both Sofia Wilén and Anna Ardin's cases at the time, had demonstratively closed the more serious part relating to Wilén, stating that 'no crime had been committed'; and she expressly ordered Gehlin to keep his 'hands off'. Nonetheless, Gehlin submitted Wilén's condom under Ardin's case number.

The lab results, available two months later, seemed to have perplexed the good inspector. He'd not asked the lab to check for DNA, only to see if they could determine how the condoms had been torn. But they did a DNA test anyway, and came up with some rather shattering results, results the Swedish media have done their best to hide from the citizenry ever since.

The condom submitted by Anna Ardin showed no traces whatsoever of chromosomal (genomic) DNA—meaning the condom cannot have been used for sex.

Designation	Object
AB/7525-10/G001	Condom Number: 2010-0201-BG20840-2 Client ID: AB/7525-10/G001 SKL number: 201001231101 Handling of materials: returned separately Methods used: B-SF02*, B-M55*, B-SF03*, B-M56*, B-M71*, B-M72*
Condom	Part of condom Number: 2010-K246314-10 Client ID: Condom SKL number: 201001231102 Handling of materials: returned separately

	Methods used: B-SF02*, B-M55*, B-SF03*, B-M56*, B-M71*, B-M72*

Objective

The objective is to investigate in which way condom AB/7525-10/G001 and the part of condom 'Condom' have been damaged.

Related Information

Investigation of damages is not part of the accreditation of the laboratory according to ISO/IEC 17025. The results of the DNA tests are returned separately.

Investigation and Conclusions

AB/7525-10/G001	Condom
Investigation of damages	Condom AB/7525-10/G001 was thoroughly damaged in the front. The edges of the damage were studied under microscope. No traces were found that could have been caused by tools. On the other hand, small scratches were found in the area close to the damaged area, perpendicular to the length of the damage. Test damage was achieved on the back part of the condom with a knife and with scissors and by ripping off the back part. The surface of the damaged area was similar to that of the torn part, whilst the surfaces damaged by the tools showed a number of small scratches. The appearance of the front torn part of the condom is seen in picture 1.

	Conclusion The results indicate that the damage in the front part of condom AB/7525-10/G001 has been achieved by tearing the condom (Grade +2).
Condom	Part of condom
Investigation of damages	The condom part 'Condom' was the front part of a condom, see picture 2. The ripped edge was studied under microscope. No traces that could have been made by tools were seen at the edges. Small scratches were observed in some areas near the ripped edge and perpendicular to the ripped edge. The appearance of the ripped edge was reminiscent of the ripped edge of condoms that were ripped in the laboratory. Conclusion The results indicate that the ripped edge of the condom part 'Condom' have been achieved by tearing the condom (Grade +2).

Investigation

Investigation	Investigator
Investigation of damages	First forensic scientist Lennart Jonasson (chief inspector) forensic scientist Bengt Forsby

Assessment Scale

SKL grade assessments on a scale from -4 to +4. The assessment given to the results for the two condoms submitted by Mats Gehlin is therefore the third highest. Following are the top assessments available from SKL.

Grade +4 — The results indicate with certainty that ...
The possibility of achieving these results if another hypothesis is true is assessed to be non-existent.

Grade +3 — The results indicate strongly that ...
The possibility of achieving these results if another hypothesis is true is assessed to be very small.

Grade +2 — The results indicate that ...
The possibility of achieving these results if another hypothesis is true is assessed to be small.

Grade +1 — The results to some extent indicate that ...
The results lend somewhat more support for the proposed hypothesis than for other hypotheses.

Grade 0 — The results are indecisive
The results do not lend more support for the proposed hypothesis than for other hypotheses.

Three Days Later

A perplexed Mats Gehlin contacted the crime lab three days later on Thursday 28 October 2010. Gehlin's report was added to the case file at 15:24 that afternoon.

Conversation with SKL

I spoke with forensic scientist Anders Nilsson at SKL to get a clarification about the results of the DNA tests.

In an earlier memo, I've written that the condom used by Anna Ardin didn't have DNA. This is not true according to Anders Nilsson. He said he saw something but couldn't make out what it was. They've decided to test the condom with a more sophisticated method. This method will take approximately two weeks. I didn't speak with Anders Nilsson last time.

Anders Nilsson explains that it's not the amount of DNA that's decisive in their ability to detect DNA. There can be many reasons they can't detect better.

- Something disturbs the analysis. Such as dirt.
- Too small quantities of DNA.
- People emit different quantities of DNA.
- The object has been altered after use by being washed, wiped off.

These were some examples of what can influence the analysis of DNA but there are further factors as well.

Mats Gehlin

Five Days Earlier

Mats Gehlin filed a separate report five days before the lab results were returned. He'd evidently been in contact with the lab at that time. His filing is stamped 15:08 20 October 2010.

A conversation with SKL yielded the following.

The condom from the residence of complainant 2 [Ardin] had no traces of DNA.

Vaginal swabs from complainant 1 had DNA from complainant 1 and a man.

The bit of condom found in the residence of complainant 1 had DNA from complainant 1 and the same man found on the vaginal swabs.

Complainant 1 did not notice that a condom broke as it was dark in the room, and when the suspect put on the condom, she heard a noise as if he were pulling on a balloon. The bit of condom was found under the bed, under the part of the bed where the suspect was lying when he put on the condom.

CHAPTER 14:
AFTER THE
INTERROGATIONS

After weeks of waiting for a chance to clear his name, Julian Assange was finally told by Marianne Ny that he could leave the country. Yet on the very day he finally left (27 September) Marianne Ny issued a secret warrant for his arrest, a warrant which should have reached all ports, including the Arlanda airport where Julian disembarked several hours later on a flight to Berlin.

But still the suspicions of a hidden agenda hadn't led to irrevocable conclusions. They were to come later in the following month.

Julian Assange was invited to speak for Afghanistan Week in ABF-huset in Stockholm in October 2010, and to march in a demonstration the following Saturday through the streets of the city. But his three laptops had been stolen from behind the Lufthansa counter at the Arlanda airport on the day of his departure, and recovering from this loss prevented him from returning in time for his scheduled speech.

Julian had of course no way of knowing at the time what he was missing.

It's been suggested a good friend alerted Julian, and that can still be the case, but the truth would seem simpler still.

Julian's Swedish legal counsel Björn Hurtig was asked to stay in his office after hours, as there was a likelihood Marianne Ny would soon have Julian in custody.

(This was to surface later when Hurtig submitted his bill to the prosecution authority and accounted for his overtime. It was corroborated by Marianne Ny's assistant Erika Leijnefors.)

Knowing that Marianne Ny had attempted to spring a trap on him, Julian thought twice about returning for the Saturday demonstration. It's apparent in retrospect that this is when he finally realised nothing was as it seemed in the Scandinavian country, and foul forces were afoot.

POSTSCRIPT:
KLARA KOPS

'Klara Kops' was an expression minted to describe the bungling efforts of the Swedish police and prosecution authority to handle the case of Julian Assange. It's of course based on the famous 'Keystone Kops' from the days of silent movies.

The story of 'Assange in Sweden' is not so much a story of Assange as it's a story of modern Sweden—the Sweden that superseded the 'golden years' of Tage Erlander and Olof Palme, when the US Republican Party gained a foothold by cultivating a young Fredrik Reinfeldt, when CIA buddy Carl Bildt was openly sending information to his friends in Langley who then, according to diplomatic cables released by WikiLeaks, concocted the big 'Russian submarine scare' of the 1980s—all the while Bildt was taking the podium in the parliament and denouncing the sitting government for 'going soft' on the Russians—all in a concerted effort to push public opinion in the country to the right and into the waiting arms of the United States.

It's a story of a woman who'd published a 'revenge plan' to use when jilted by a lover—a woman with mysterious ties to strange organisations.

It's a story of how, on word of mouth alone, the prosecutor-on-duty at one of Stockholm's most trafficked police stations issued a warrant in absentia in a case where there still hadn't been any formal testimony, on the grounds that foreigners could skip the country— only for this same prosecutor to spill the beans to the tabloids, thereby undermining her own stated intentions.

It's a story of how this 'Klara Kops' police station, one of the busiest in the country, sitting atop the biggest train station in the country, with strict orders to make video recordings of all testimony in all cases of this nature, suddenly had no video equipment available, professedly had no audio equipment available either, and yet, using a 'conceptual format', took down the words of witnesses anyway, interpreting those words as they went on.

It's a story of how a few Swedish journalists decided to 'out' Julian

Assange, despite clear rules of ethics against such willful defamation—possibly because they intuitively realised, from their editor-in-chief on down, that they'd stumbled onto the biggest scoop in their publishing history.

It's a story of how one of the country's premier advocates of 'politically correct' went on national television and instructed the citizenry to not think about the puzzling case.

It's a story of how one lawyer possibly saw a chance to make a career comeback, and petitioned to have a case that had been dropped reopened—something even the women making the accusations didn't know was possible.

It's a story of a country long famous for its equality between the sexes, where equality has long since ceased to be an issue, and where radical feminist conventions regularly end their meetings with chants about how they're going to dismember and hang all men.

It's a story of a country with a long and unmatched history of miscarriages and travesties of justice, created by a flimsy judicial system where court judges most often have no education in the law whatsoever, and by powerful media organisations intent only on increasing their readership, damn the torpedoes and the innocents.

It's a story of a country completely out of control, where a serial killer turned out to be no more than an institutionalised and drugged-out victim of authorities who were the really crazy ones.

It's a story of radical 'feminism' so out of control that clinics in the capital regularly issue 'rape certificates' based not on forensic science but on what the 'patients'—and above all the doctors—*feel*.

It's a story of a small country where everyone knows everyone, and everyone knows how the game is really played; so it's no surprise that most of the evils exposed never get legs, because those in power always know someone who can stop the stories from spreading (as in the above case of the fake 'rape certificates' where the husband of the doctor in question is the head legal counsel for the country's biggest news organisation).

It's a story ripe with the stench of collusion. A collusion shared by the United Kingdom and Australia, and against a man and his organisation that otherwise enjoy unparalleled international renown.

It's a story that would never have been told if Julian Assange hadn't returned to Sweden on Wednesday 11 August 2010.

This book is planned as the first in a series.

The truth will out, the truth wins out.

Stockholm/London 19 February 2013

Apparently Swedish laws are unique. If you have a penis you're half a rapist before you even get through customs.
   - Scott Adams

If I am able to reveal what I know, everyone will realise this is all a charade. If I could tell the British courts, I suspect it would make extradition a moot point.
   - Björn Hurtig

I can tell you that the Swedish prosecution still hasn't provided copies of those SMS texts that have been referred to. Those texts are some of the most powerful exculpatory evidence. In Australia prosecutors have a very grave duty to disclose such evidence to courts when seeking the grave exercise of a court's power against an individual. Yet in Sweden in this case, in the first hearings to obtain an arrest warrant, those texts were not submitted to the Swedish court, which is highly improper.
   - James Catlin

ABOUT THE AUTHORS

Members of the Radsoft team of software developers were burning the midnight oil on the morning of 21 August 2010 when they saw the *Expressen* story break. They and their associates at Rixstep, another software consultant company, have been on the story of Assange in Sweden ever since. Some who had lived in Sweden were puzzled at the way the case was being handled by the Swedish authorities and the Swedish media, and decided to investigate. As some of the team members are also professional translators, they decided to help bring the Assange story to a wider audience by translating these documents into English.

Bridget Hunter is a professional editor based in the UK.

www.ingramcontent.com/pod-product-compliance
Lightning Source LLC
Chambersburg PA
CBHW050442290526
45786CB00006B/2122